# STOP SELLING AND START CLOSING

Master Psychological Sales Motivators to Know and Not Hope for the Close

Michael W Steiger

**Steiger**

Copyright © 2024 Michael W Steiger

All rights reserved

No part of this book may be reproduced, or stored in a retrieval system, or transmitted in any form or by any means, electronic, mechanical, photocopying, recording, or otherwise, without express written permission of the publisher.

ISBN: 978-1-0688728-1-5

Cover design by: Steiger
Send questions to michaelwsteiger@gmaill.com.

# STOP SELLING AND START CLOSING.

Learn how to stop selling, start Closing, and earn more by turning customers into clients as you guide them to a valuable exchange of their hard-earned money to satisfy their wants and desires.

This is your practical guide to sales and negotiation. Here you will learn about the psychological motivators and inhibitors of a customer. You will learn to use these motivations to help guide a customer to realize their true desires. You will learn powerful tried and true techniques, so that you can confidently lead the customer to Closing on their wants and desires.

Knowing that you will make the sale and not just wish for it.

By Michael W. Steiger

# CONTENTS

Title Page
Copyright
Stop selling and start Closing.
SECTION 1: INTRODUCTION   1
The One-time Payment Sale.   3
My Education In Sales.   4
Closing vs Selling.   6
Sales are the backbone of the economy.   7
A felt need, that the customer must justify logically.   8
Their money is safest in their wallet. Part 1.   10
You don't want friends, you want clients.   12
My biggest pet peeve is not being Closed.   13
You can be great. That is why you are here.   14
What I want for you.   15
Practice! Practice! Practice!   16
Start Closing, stop selling.   17
SECTION 2: CLIENT MOTIVATIONS   18
Ask for the Close.   19
Their money is safest in their wallet. Part 2.   20
Think of yourself as the assistant buyer.   21
Treat everyone as if they have the ability to buy. Treat everyone as a buyer.   22

| | |
|---|---|
| Do not sell with your own wallet. | 24 |
| One is actually Three. | 25 |
| To be convincing you must be convinced of your own products or services. | 26 |
| They aren't "Window Shopping", they are doing research. | 27 |
| The objections you get are probably something you believe. | 29 |
| I don't know. Part 1. | 30 |
| Do not argue. | 31 |
| Go for it, what do you have to lose? | 32 |
| SECTION 3: BASIC TECHNIQUES 1 | 33 |
| Ask for the Close. | 34 |
| Learn their name. | 35 |
| Never answer their questions. Well not until later anyway. Part 1. | 37 |
| Never answer their questions. Well not until later anyway. Part 2 | 42 |
| SECTION 4: BASIC TECHNIQUES 2 | 44 |
| Tell me about….. | 45 |
| Learn their language. | 46 |
| Sell their service. Not your Service. | 48 |
| Tell them their story again and again. | 50 |
| Tell me what you have learned already. | 52 |
| Customer keeps moving the target around. | 54 |
| Never ever say the words Buy or Cost. | 55 |
| Never say "But". Use "However". | 57 |
| There are no Dumb Questions. | 59 |
| The client may not know what they really want, because they don't know what's really out there. | 61 |
| Low Middle High. | 63 |

| | |
|---|---:|
| You never get more by paying less. Part 1. | 65 |
| You never get more by paying less. Part 2. | 68 |
| I understand. Can you share with me your concerns? | 69 |
| Dealing with the EXPERT. Part 1. | 70 |
| Dealing with the EXPERT. Part 2. | 73 |
| Dealing with the EXPERT. Part 3. | 74 |
| Never use the phrases "To be honest with you" or "Trust me". | 76 |
| When they already know what they want. | 78 |
| Sometimes customers just suck. | 79 |
| Intensify the desire to buy. | 81 |
| SECTION 5: ADVANCED TECHNIQUES | 82 |
| What is the Advanced Secret Technique? | 83 |
| How to Say Hello. | 84 |
| Hello Part 1: To say Hello. Or not to say hello. That is the question. | 85 |
| Hello Part 2: Hello through geography. | 87 |
| Hello Part 3: What's got you stopping by? | 89 |
| Hello Part 4: Doing a little research? | 91 |
| Hello Part 5: The Secretary introduction. | 92 |
| Hello Part 6: The Feint. | 94 |
| Saying hello in the outside world. | 96 |
| Smiling. | 97 |
| Drop the fake enthusiasm. | 100 |
| People love to hear themselves talk. | 102 |
| Always be Closing. Part 1. | 104 |
| Always be Closing. Part 2. | 105 |
| Why would you buy that? | 106 |
| Never directly say that you are better than the | 108 |

competition.

| | |
|---|---|
| Directly tell them you are better than the competition. | 109 |
| If the client actually thought the competition was better they would've already gone with them. | 111 |
| I don't know. Part 2. | 112 |
| Do not argue. | 114 |
| Complaints. Sometimes, it's just a complaint. Get over it and move on. | 116 |
| The price is a benefit. | 120 |
| Sell them, don't let them sell you. | 123 |
| Always upsell. | 125 |
| Don't miss an opportunity. | 127 |
| Let's talk to the "Expert". | 129 |
| Because. | 132 |
| Try one more time. | 135 |
| SECTION 6: PRICE NEGOTIATIONS | 136 |
| When possible, negotiate by moving down a product line. | 137 |
| Reduce a client's fear of money. Make it easy for the client to buy. | 138 |
| Create value. Justify with a financial value multiplier. | 141 |
| I have no more money to give you. | 143 |
| SECTION 7: CLOSES | 144 |
| Shall We? | 145 |
| Who's name? | 146 |
| Go for it! | 147 |
| Treat yourself. | 148 |
| Do it Anyway. | 149 |
| You cant take it with you. | 150 |
| Haven't you already thought about it? | 151 |

| | |
|---|---|
| Because. | 152 |
| I understand. | 153 |
| Ask for forgiveness. | 154 |
| Why? | 155 |
| Your money is safe in your wallet. | 156 |
| Summary | 159 |
| Afterword | 161 |

# SECTION 1: INTRODUCTION

## You Are The Frontline.

Hello.

For those of you here new to sales. Welcome to your new life in sales. May it be exciting and successful. In the pages presented here my goal is to help you learn techniques and psychology that will not only help you to succeed, but to excel on the front lines of your new sales career.

For those of you here, that have been selling for a few years already, but want more from your time spent on the sales floor. These pages will present a deeper understanding of what is happening between you and your client and how to Close them.

For those old pros. May this course help you refresh, refine and sharpen your current techniques.

I am writing this book to teach a salesperson to become a sale's Closer. To be the best at your craft. Let me be clearer. **I want you to stop selling products or services and start CLOSING on the opportunities presented while engaged with a client, searching for clues, looking to satisfy their Wants and Desires.**

What I will present here is a refined learning experience. A practical guide to sales through the psychology of a sale and the techniques that you can use to Close the sale.

This manual is compiled from my years of experience in sales, refined by knowledge gained through applying the lessons I have learned while actively engaged in the sales and Closing process. From those personal learning experiences gained through both triumph and tragedy, I present here proven techniques and psychologies that I have honed to work on the showroom floor while actively engaged with a client. What you will learn here can be immediately deployed to improve your sales experience.

# THE ONE-TIME PAYMENT SALE.

Our focus in this manual's lessons will be on the *One-time Payment Sale.* **The One on One, on the Showroom Floor, Retail Sales level engagement. Where you want the client to walk away with your goods and services today.**

When I refer to the One-time Payment Sale or Retail Sales. We are talking about a client that will be paying by Cash, Check or Credit. The client will be making one or at the most two payments for the products or services that they desire. Possibly a deposit and a final payment. We will treat these as one payment as often they are just a formality. What we will not be relying on are financed payments or mortgaged loans to help finalize a sale.

Financed payment based sales have an edge that can be relied on to Close the sale. I have found that most of the education about sales focuses on this edge. Financed payment based sales are very effective when available. But these sales are a crutch and often not available to most salespeople. There will be no crutch for us here. We are going to look at what I believe is the purer form of sales.

# MY EDUCATION IN SALES.

As a student of the Art of Sales I devoured all the books on the subject I could find. However I found that the available education about sales to be lacking in focus for the bringing to a Close, the *One-Time Payment Sale*. My goal here in the following pages of this manual is to provide this focused education. The hard earned education and insights I gained from applying the lessons that I had to dig out of the books written by the Great Sales Educators that I looked to for inspiration. Then through the many hours of direct interactions with clients honing and refining what I have learned through both triumph and failure into a powerful understanding of the psychology of sales and the techniques used to bring them to a valuable Close for both you and your new clients.

As great as the original sales educators may be at teaching sales. I have found that the writing in their books has a frame of reference coming from their time in sales. Their frame of reference often coming from selling of real estate, vehicles or large contracts often involving long term payment financing or a mortgaged loan. So the education in sales they provide focuses on Closing these types of sales.

But let me ask you. What sounds more difficult selling a Luxury Item like a Home Theater System for $250,000 with the swipe of a credit card, or the sale of a High End automobile with monthly installments spread out over time to take away the pain of the hit to the customer's finances?

I am going to give you tried and true techniques to deal with this Retail level One-Time Payment sale. I want you to feel as confident and stress free selling a $100 Bluetooth speaker or a

$250,000 home theater system. In these pages you will come to understand the psychological motivations and motivators of a sale. You will know how to guide a client in acquiring your offerings, whether it be a Timex or a Rolex. You will be able to Close them on their wants, needs and desires.

# CLOSING VS SELLING.

We are going to learn to **Close** in the following lessons presented here. You are no longer going to **Sell** something; you are going to **Close** a sale. And there is a huge difference between Closing a sale and Selling.

Selling is what a website does. A website shows you a bunch of pretty pictures and with some information to read, hoping you will buy. A fast food restaurant Sells food. They present a menu, you make your choices and they sell you the food.

A **Close**r identifies a client's wants and desires. Knowingly and skillfully helps the client to act on those desires, all the while moving them towards a final exchange of value for their hard-earned money, for your goods and services.

You are not presenting a product and asking a customer to buy it. Your job. No, it's not a job. It's a duty. It is your duty. It is your duty to the client to help guide them. They have a want, you have to help them in justifying this want and urge so that they go home with the object of their desires. We are here together to develop your skills as a Closer, so that you will know, not wish, that they will go home with your products or services.

Stop selling. Start **Closing**. Let me teach you how.

# SALES ARE THE BACKBONE OF THE ECONOMY.

Nothing in this world will happen or start without the Closing of a sale or idea.

Sales are the backbone of the free enterprise system. Without a sale there is no exchange, therefore no value is created. Without a valuable creation, there will be no currency exchanged for that value. And you will have earned nothing for your time.

Sales are why you are here. Sales and the exchange of money for an item of value is why there is a company for you to work for. Sales might be why you have a company. Sales are why you get paid. A Closed sale for an exchange of value is the line between success and failure. And in sales you cannot have too many failures before the job, the paycheck, the company and the economy are gone for good.

To be blunt. You do not pay the bills with good intentions. Yes, you can make friends. You can make great presentations. You can act with empathy and feel morally confident that you provide great service to your fellow man. But if you do not Close the deal and you don't satisfy the customer's needs. There will be no sale and you will provide no value to yourself or your company.

# A FELT NEED, THAT THE CUSTOMER MUST JUSTIFY LOGICALLY.

When a customer decides that they want something. It usually starts with a felt need or a sudden desire. It may only take them a day or two to take action but often it takes months or sometimes years for them to act on this "sudden" desire. When they finally reach you. When they make the journey to your showroom floor, your job will be to help them Logically justify this Need, this felt Desire. You will become their guide. Helping them to deepen this desire and lead them to a logical understanding of why they should own this desire and make the purchase. But if you only increase their desires without helping them come to a logical justification for that desire. You will most likely lose out the Close. Or worse they will make a purchase, only to have buyers remorse and attempt to return the purchase.

In every client there are two competing sides in their mind, when they are considering a purchase. They have a Feeling side and a Logical side. When they develop a desire for something. That desire builds in the feeling side of their brain. When they get this Feeling this Desire, it's at this time the logical side of their brain kicks in. The Logical side of their brain will literally try to crush their Felt Needs by providing the reasons not to buy. And it is very good at this. The logical side wants to be "safe" with the money. This is when the customer needs your help and guidance. The Feeling side of their brain will hardly need a push towards their desires. The Logical side truly wants and needs you to help rationalize these Wants and Desires.

This War Between the Desire and Logic can not be

underestimated. This may be the most important part of what you learn here. Understanding this is crucial to helping a customer Close on a sale.

**They want it!** This does not mean they will get it! Maybe the rational side of their brain has a better argument against the purchase. It's probably not a better argument, it's just a rationalization to feel safe. This is your primary purpose. Help them, guide them, make them feel safe and secure when they finally decide to purchase.

Remember this always. **The rational side is always defending the money, however, people have wants and they want to get the things that they want.**

# THEIR MONEY IS SAFEST IN THEIR WALLET. PART 1.

Protect the money. This is the primary mandate of the customer's logical side of their brain.

Today more than ever people do not like to make a decision. I find people are growing more and more indecisive than ever before. Even with the strongest of desires. The logical mind can stop a potential customer from deciding to purchase. The quantity of information and opinions out in the World and on the Web is staggering. What comes from all of these opinions, and the unending pages of information on the Web is pure noise. In that noise the negative will be easier to understand. The logical mind will find that negative info as a reason to not purchase. It will protect the money and keep it "safe" in their wallet.

From this noise comes the fear of making a bad decision with their money. This fear has grown to levels unprecedented in the history of sales. With this fear they learn that their money is safest in their wallet.

The logical side soothes them and tells them they are safe, and their money is safe. This safety becomes an anchor against deciding. It will lock them down. They will not make a decision. There will not be a valuable exchange of your goods and services for their hard-earned money.

Without an exchange of value. The customer does not get what they want, and then you and your company do not prosper.

Overcoming a customer's fear is your primary purpose as a professional in sales. It is your solemn duty to your client to help them Close.

# YOU DON'T WANT FRIENDS, YOU WANT CLIENTS.

You are not here to make friends. **You are here to create great client relationships that result in the Close.** Look if all we were here to do was make friends. Then this game would be easy. You are here to earn a client. Hopefully a long lasting one.

Can you be friendly with customers? Can customers become friends? Yes.

But friendship is not the goal here.

**The goal is to develop a strong, Ethical Relationship with your client.** A relationship that helps them get what they want and need. So that you can get what you want and need. The Close.

So, I am not saying that you are not allowed to like your clients, or that it does not matter if they like you as a person. Let me be clear. You are here to get a customer to become your client. And you want and need them to see you as their advisor. You want clients coming to you when they make a purchase. Gaining a "friend" does not help. It does not help your bottom line. It does not help your company. It will not get you noticed by management. "Friends" do not pay the bills. Clients who will Close do. Turn customers into clients. Help your clients Close.

# MY BIGGEST PET PEEVE IS NOT BEING CLOSED.

This is really a personal note. I write this coming from my past experiences as a customer.

My biggest pet peeve is not being Closed when I want something. I absolutely hate not being Closed when I want something. Yes, my money may be safe for the proverbial rainy day. But I had the money. I had the desire. I wanted to exchange my money for the goods and services I desired. I was more than likely ready to spend even more of that hard-earned money then I had planned for, going well beyond my original budget. I, like many other customers, had spent hour upon hour researching and agonizing over some object of desire that I felt a need for. I had found a showroom and took my limited available time to go to that showroom. Only to leave without.

Take a moment to think about all the times you left a showroom without. You wanted it. Why didn't you buy it?

When we as salespeople do not learn what a customer's wants and needs are, and then fail to help them justify those wants and needs, we truly let them down.

Do not let them down.

## YOU CAN BE GREAT. THAT IS WHY YOU ARE HERE.

**"Believe in your own greatness."** This is a powerful quote that has stuck with me over the years. Repeat it. Take it to heart. See yourself as great and you will be great.

Look, do you want to be noticed at work? Maybe you work in a place that has global commissions. Or no commission. How do you move ahead? Sales. If you start Closing more sales, you will get noticed.

Your job is to sell more. Help customers buy more. Be the reason why the store succeeds. Get noticed. This is what your job is. This is your goal. This is your obligation to yourself, to your store, and to your family.

Do you want to be the manager that one day trains the people on the floor? Prove to those around you that you have what it takes to succeed on the floor and Close the sale. Help your customers make an exchange and Close the sale.

Look here. You are always and will always be selling in your life. Do you want the girl, the job, the part in the play? Do you want to convince a person or people to follow your plan? Do you want them to adopt your ideas and to follow your lead? You must sell them on you, your ideas, and your plans. Don't like this. Well too bad. Now go after what you want. Straight ahead. Go right for the prize. Be great. Believe in your own greatness.

# WHAT I WANT FOR YOU.

Confidence. I want to help you grow in the confidence of your skills. A confidence developed through internalizing the techniques and coming to know a deeper understanding of the psychology of Closing a client presented here in this manual.

I want you to be able to flawlessly use these techniques and be able to fall back on them at any time. Techniques sharpened into a formidable understanding of how to lead the client with an array of Closing Skills.

Over time and with practice, the techniques and psychology presented here will become internalized and customized into your own personal style. These techniques will continue to grow over your sales career in effectiveness. With this growing skill set comes a confidence to engage with any potential client.

This is what I want for you. So practice, practice, practice.

# PRACTICE! PRACTICE! PRACTICE!

In the pages of this manual presented here I will introduce to you a new set of skills and a deeper understanding. I want you to practice these techniques. Ingrain the ideas into your very soul. Read and re-read the sections.

You must practice. You must practice continuously. You must learn these techniques, so they become a part of you and in turn an unconscious part of your delivery. Work hard at it so that when you engage with the client your words come with fluidity and without hesitation.

I want you to be able to move in and out each technique smoothly. Learning from a client and leading them to a final Yes. My goal is that one day a client looks right at you and says. "You're really good at this."

For those of you working in a retail sales position on a salary without commission, this is an ideal time for you to learn, and it's an ideal time for you to experiment. Be Brave.

Here is another "take it to heart" from me to you. With your new successes, you will have failures. From your failures can come the best lessons and your strongest motivations. I want you to look at your failures and ask yourself "why did I fail?". Examine the failure and feel the pain of it. Turn the pain from your loss, because you have lost, into a new drive, and a strengthened desire for success. Honestly look to yourself, see where you went wrong and turn the failure into a lesson to succeed.

## START CLOSING, STOP SELLING.

You are not here to learn to sell. You are here to learn to Close. So again. A commercial on television sells a product. The man behind the counter at your favorite fast food joint is selling. You are Closing. Your client needs you to Close them on their wants and desires.

# SECTION 2: CLIENT MOTIVATIONS

What is motivating the client? What is stopping the client from moving forward? How do you help them?

# ASK FOR THE CLOSE.

First and foremost, if you want to motivate a customer. Ask For the Close. You are going to see this stressed more than a few times throughout this sales manual. I cannot stress this enough. I see it so often. Salespeople that will simply not ask the customer to Close the sale.

I can still remember the times early in my career where I was locked up, and too insecure to ask for the sale. Thankfully I had someone teach me to have courage and turn my fears into motivations.

Ask for the Close. So many sales people go through great lengths to build rapport, give a great demo, and answer all of the client's questions. Only to fall short in the end. They do not ask for the Close. They do not ask for the exchange. They do not get to realise any value for what they have done. It's one thing to lose a sale for reasons outside of your control. But to never have asked for it in the first place is by far the worst outcome.

# THEIR MONEY IS SAFEST IN THEIR WALLET. PART 2.

This is the underlying tenet of everything you will learn here. They as a client and you as a salesperson are always struggling against this safety. The money is locked in but it wants out. And believe me when I say this, "the client wants to give it to you".

They have a felt want. A desire. So, we are going to grow that desire. Intensify it. Then justify it. Together you and the client will pick that lock and open that wallet.

People are often very insecure about their money. The nicest thing you can do is help them make a decision. They will thank you for it.

# THINK OF YOURSELF AS THE ASSISTANT BUYER.

Think of yourself as an Assistant buyer to the client. Be ethical and work with your client sincerely and honestly with their best interest in mind. As their assistant buyer it's your job to help them to justify the purchase. Without justification their money will stay sitting safe in their wallet. So, help them intensify the felt need that they have. Assist them with justifying the Close.

Be your best self. Believe in your product and services. Assist and guide your client. They need you.

## TREAT EVERYONE AS IF THEY HAVE THE ABILITY TO BUY. TREAT EVERYONE AS A BUYER.

Treat everyone as a buyer. In both spirit and means. Treat them as if they have the means to make an exchange of value and the willingness to do so. Believe in them and they will believe in themselves.

This should be your core belief about a potential client. And I can tell you from experience it is true.

When you treat customers as if they are going to make a purchase. They will. And if you make assumptions about them in a negative light. They won't. And worse, maybe they will, but it will not be from you.

Here are two of the basic mistakes that a salesperson can make related to a potential client's ability to make a purchase.

One of the biggest mistake's salesperson can make is to judge a potential client on the way they look. This is a huge mistake. Especially early in your career. **You cannot tell a book by its cover.**

For example, if a person enters my showroom and they look dirty and grubby. I always take a deeper look. Where some might just immediately blow the potential off. I try to look deeper. Is that grease? Is that paint? He may have a business that requires him to use his hands. And I can tell you some people make a great living with their hands. So don't be quick to judge on appearance. Treat him as a buyer and you may find out that he is going to make your day.

The second big mistake. And this is the biggest mistake you can make as a salesperson. You believe the client when they tell you they can't or won't buy. Trusting them when they tell you they can't afford the purchase, or that the price is too high, or any other excuse they come up with. That's on you. Remember this, the logical side of their brain will say anything to protect the money in their wallet. Your believing them, for whatever excuse they give you, will be your failure to assist them with the Close.

Both mistakes reflect on you.

Learn to be confident in the client's ability to make a purchase. See everyone as a buyer.

# DO NOT SELL WITH YOUR OWN WALLET.

Don't sell with your own wallet. Have you ever heard this before? Well learn it. And learn it well. I have sold items that were so far beyond my means that they would seem like mythical dreams to most people. But my means are not my client's means. To them, the exchange of large sums of cash gets them what they want and desire. Just because you cannot pay for it with your wallet, does not mean that they can't and won't pay with it with their wallet. This is why I always sell upwards and so should you. Believe in their ability to make that purchase.

Conversely, Never look negatively upon a person who simply cannot afford it. Never embarrass them for this. Treat them well. Maybe one day they will be able to make that purchase. You want them to come looking for you.

# ONE IS ACTUALLY THREE.

Here is a general rule of thumb. If a customer tells you that they have one dollar, they actually have three. This is why you should always sell up. Always move the client up before moving the client down.

When the client tells you that they only have one dollar or that they are only willing to spend one dollar, I want you to disregard this. Acknowledge it, but move past it. That dollar is just the starting point.

Remember that logical side of the customer's brain. The side that is protecting the money. It's in your showroom right now because it's a little curious about this desire coming from the otherside of the customer's brain. It's basically agreed to come in for a look. It needs some information. Maybe to squash this desire or maybe to move forward. The dollar is a test point. To the logical side, what a dollar will acquire is probably good enough. The logical side is protecting the other two dollars at the moment.

So when you are engaged with a customer, take opportunities that come to move them up. Moving them up can and will increase their desire. You need to show them what the extra two dollars can mean in benefits to them. They may not even know that there is a next level or how truly awesome the next level is. You will be doing them a great favor by educating them in the possibilities. Of course you will need to continue to help the customer justify the desire.

One interesting note here is that sometimes the move up is the justification.

## TO BE CONVINCING YOU MUST BE CONVINCED OF YOUR OWN PRODUCTS OR SERVICES.

It is a good idea to own or use the products and services you sell. If you believe in them enough to own them yourself it will come across in your presentations.

Maybe you are selling something so far out of your current abilities to afford it. Maybe it is a dream of yours to own it. Maybe it's why you have ended up working there. Then I say be a fan. Be a huge fan. Get behind your products, and dream big. Learn to extol their virtues and yearn to benefit from their virtues. Share this dream with your clients. And one day you will be an owner not just a seller.

The thing is, when you believe in your own products and services, it will be hard for you to understand why a customer says no to you. Not being able to understand why they would say no is a good belief. Be excited. Because the more you believe in the products and services you represent, the less customers will say no to you and start saying yes.

## THEY AREN'T "WINDOW SHOPPING", THEY ARE DOING RESEARCH.

No one is ever just "Window Shopping". They are always shopping. They are doing the research. Maybe they are not buying today. But there is a good chance they will buy eventually. This is where your help and guidance will come in.

Take a moment to think about this. Have you ever personally gone window shopping for something that you weren't interested in. Exactly. Why would you? When you have that sudden urge, you need to know more. So, when they say that they are just Window Shopping, I want you to translate this as, they have felt a desire and now need more information. The research that they are doing while they are just window shopping will help them justify this desire.

"I am just Window Shopping" is a customer saying to you, "please leave me alone, I am not quite ready yet". You leaving them alone is what the customer thinks they want you to do. But stop for a moment. Listen to what I am saying. **They are not talking to you, they are talking to themselves.** The desire they feel is real. But, remember, the Wallet. "I am just window shopping" is a defense mechanism from the rational side of their brain.

Remember your duty to them.

And to help you in this duty. You are going to learn in the *Advanced Techniques* section of this manual, how to maneuver past this defense. Because, how can you help them if they won't let you. You are going to learn how to properly say "Hello" to a customer. You are going to learn to engage them in ways that will get past their barriers or even stop them from erecting them in the first place.

So, remember they are just protecting their wallet. But I can tell you that often this Window Shopper has spent hours online already. They probably know the product inside and out. I have often found that their knowledge on a particular product can outweigh my own. They have researched it deeply. They are in your showroom. Help them.

# THE OBJECTIONS YOU GET ARE PROBABLY SOMETHING YOU BELIEVE.

Sometimes in sales, there will be objections you receive from a client that you cannot overcome. And it may be hard for you to understand why it was so easy for the objection to stall or even cancel the sale.

But maybe it's not the objection. Maybe it's You.

If an objection has that much power that it can destroy a sale for you. Then, the objection was probably something that you also believe to be true. Even if you do not believe the objection on the surface, you may have an agreement with the objection subconsciously.

This issue. And we will call it an issue here. This issue needs to get sorted out immediately in your head. This belief in this objection on your part, is very much related to the two ideas of *not selling with your own wallet* and *that you must be convinced of your products and services value*.

So be careful.

If you believe that the objection outweighs the benefits of your products or services. The objection will be hard if not impossible to overcome.

If you personally believe that the benefits outweigh the objections. It will be easy to move past the objections and help the client receive those benefits.

# I DON'T KNOW. PART 1.

"I don't know". Learn this phrase. And rely on it. It will save you one day.

This is straightforward advice. Never tell a client anything that you do not know for sure is the verifiable truth. **It is ok to tell a client you don't know the answer.**

A client will take even the slightest grain of any remark you make, even remarks made off hand as the absolute gospel truth. Never over promise. Never make false statements. Never say anything you cannot back up.

When things go sideways, and inevitably you will have something go wrong or not work exactly like you stated it would, the clients will latch onto your statements. Whether the client remembers what you said rightly or wrongly, what you said can and will come back to destroy you.

And I mean destroy. Some clients out there are very unethical in how they approach sales. Remember this, they see you as only wanting their money. So, if things go wrong. They will try to get everything they can out of you.

So be careful.

To finish off this section, here is some advice from me to you. If you and a client have a conversation. And some information is shared. It's a good idea to send them an email confirming the points of the conversation. And don't forget to ask for confirmation that they have received the email. Trust me. One day it will come in handy.

# DO NOT ARGUE.

Do not argue with a client. It will get you nowhere.

You will never get a person to change their mind through argument. However you can help them to come to a new decision based on new facts.

It is better to let them present their facts. Don't argue. Just learn what they are.

Later we will learn how to use "I may be wrong", "I don't know", or "I agree" to present new facts, to bond with the client, and move the sale towards a Close.

# GO FOR IT, WHAT DO YOU HAVE TO LOSE?

This almost sounds like a Close you would use on a customer. But I am telling you to go for it. What do you have to lose?

I'll tell you what you have to lose.

What you have to lose is the Close! You fail your customer and lose the sale.

So drop your ego and your pride. Be brave. Overcome your fears and go for it.

So let's dive into the next section of this manual and start to learn the basic techniques of sales and start Closing.

# SECTION 3: BASIC TECHNIQUES 1

## The Foundation Stones For Your New Sales Skills.

With these foundation skills, you will be able to immediately start improving your interactions with the customers that come into your showroom, and then help them to Close on their desires.

# ASK FOR THE CLOSE.

This is the basic technique. Even a newbie on their first day on the sales floor can do it.

Ask for the Close.

Again. And I cannot say this enough. **Ask for the Close**.

So many sales people go to great lengths to build rapport with the client, give the client a great demo, and answer all of their questions, only to not fulfill the final step. They don't ask for the sale. They don't make an exchange of value with the Client. They do not get to realise any value in what they have done.

It's one thing to lose a sale. But to never have asked for it in the first place is worse.

Basic technique number 1. Ask for the Close.

# LEARN THEIR NAME.

Learn the customer's name if you want them to become a client. You will build comfort and repour quicker using their name. A person's name is magical to them. People feel important when they hear their name spoken out loud.

To not learn their name is one of the biggest mistakes you can make. I want you to see it like this. When you do not take the time to learn their name. You don't care about them. They are simply there to be taken advantage of.

So, learn their name early and use it as often as you can, and as appropriately as you can without overdoing it.

Using the client's name to build rapport and earn their trust, can take you far, while you are helping them to Close on your goods and services.

Here is a great example of this that worked on me in the past. I know how it felt personally and how positively it affected me. One of my clients would use this on me, and he was very good at it. When he learned my name, he never forgot it. And never forgot to use it. He would use it liberally when asking questions and discussing his current needs. I can tell you, I was conscious of his actions, but the effect on me was still the same. It made me feel good about myself and he usually ended up having a few points shaved off his purchases because of it. I simply could not stop myself from treating him better. All because he learned my name.

So, remember to learn the customer's name right away and then use it a few times. Try to use it again and again, nothing sounds more magical to a person than their own name.

We will learn in Advanced techniques how to actually say Hello. So, you can get a chance to learn their name.

# NEVER ANSWER THEIR QUESTIONS. WELL NOT UNTIL LATER ANYWAY. PART 1.

So here we go. You have a customer standing in front of you, on your showroom floor and they are going to start asking you questions.

Now hold tight a moment. **Do not answer the questions directly**.

Well, not until you know what the **Real Answers Are,** to their questions.

And how will you know what the answers are? You will know the answers by asking them what they are.

You may be so full of knowledge, and you may know your products inside and out. And because you want to show them you are the right guy to ask these questions, there can be a tendency to just unload your knowledge on them. They ask. You answer. But you shouldn't. And after this you won't. Because you don't know the real answers yet.

What I am a getting at here is this. **Ask them questions. A lot of questions.** You must ask as many questions as possible before presenting any information about your offerings.

So, when they ask you a question. Go ahead and ask it right back. This is one of your strongest and most important techniques in Closing a client. You will eventually find out what they really want. What their true desire is. And how to guide them to the Close.

This is the basic technique in sales. Second only to asking for the

Close. You can always come back to asking a question instead of blurting out an answer.

The power of the Question is three-fold:

One. Questions can help you to find out what is motivating the client.

Two. It helps you to find the right answers for their questions.

Three. You can use a question to build desire and help a client move towards the Close.

Let us try an example. They may ask you a simple question like "What color does it come in?". Seems like a simple question. Doesn't it? I know you want to tell them. But this is not a simple question at all. This question and others like it can stop the sale dead in its tracks. Do not answer it. Wouldn't you rather know what color they really want? How are you going to Close them if you don't know what they want? So instead of answering them with what might be the wrong answer. Find out what color they really want.

The customer asks.

"What colors does it come in?"

You ask them something like these examples.

"What color do you see it in?"

"May I ask what color you were looking for?"

"What color would match your…(living room, dress, car, ect)?"

"Please tell me. When you arrive at the event. What color do you see yourself wearing as you walk through the doors?"

Where their question was simple, but could possibly lead you to catastrophe, your question has power. It opens them up and should hopefully start them talking. We want them talking. If they are slow to start. Keep coaxing them out of their shell. As they talk, you listen and learn, so you can start building up the Justifications for their Desires.

Now did you notice the desire building in those questions? This can be the real power of questioning. When you ask them a question like "What color do you see it in?" They will automatically see it in their mind. Especially if you tell them too.

For example.

"Please tell me. In your living room. What color do you see it in?"

"Imagine you're having a party. What color would be perfect?"

"May I ask you, when you first thought about it. What did it look like? What color was it?"

Whenever possible try to ask questions that provide you with answers and at the same time build desire in the client. With practice it will become a very natural habit for you. After a while you won't know you are even doing it.

A nice side effect of questioning the client and allowing them to talk is rapport building. Because they are talking, and you are listening. They can't help themselves from not getting to like you. People like to be heard, and feel good when they know someone cares about what they are saying. No one listens anymore. They are just often waiting for their turn to speak. So ask questions and listen.

Here is one more example for you. In this example we are trying to learn a little about the client's level of experience and what they may know already. It will help you find out where their head is at. In this example the client is looking to build a home theater in the basement of their home. Your showroom may sell $1000 systems or maybe it sells $100,000 systems. These can be two vastly different clients. Or maybe it's the same client asking for a $1000 system, however he can afford the $100,000 system and will want to go that high, he simply doesn't know that the premium levels are available.

They ask. "Do you sell Home Theaters?". And of course in this example, the answer is "Yes". And they are probably going to ask "what kind do you sell" or "how much do they cost" right away.

Stop right there.

Those are very open ended questions. You need to find out a couple of things first. Lets see where their head is at and try to get a feel for their experience level. In this situation we would ask questions like these.

"Do you currently have a home theater?"

"May I ask, how do you watch movies currently?"

"Do you know what ATMOS is?" (or fill in any new or current technology)

"Do you know any of our brands?"

"What research have you done already?"

"Does one of your friends have a Home Theater system?"

See what I am doing here. They have come in off the street. You know nothing about them. They hit you with very general questions. By turning their questions around and probing them for answers, you can pick up a lot of valuable information.

From here you should be able to establish their experience level. Which will inform you how much education you will need to provide so that they understand what is being discussed. You can start to estimate how high or low you should take their budget.

With this knowledge it will be easier to start asking Desire Building Questions that will help lead your new client to the Close of the Sale.

So. Ask questions. Then ask more questions. Then ask more questions. Do not answer until you know what the answer is!

This is the most important lesson that you can learn. This is the foundation stone upon which all else lies.

Now go back and re re-read this section again.

Here is an exercise to help you build your questioning skills. Every time someone asks you a question, and I mean anyone (friends, family, coworkers), try to turn their question into a thoughtful question for them. Try to turn as many questions as you can back into a question for them. Keep count and try to beat your last record. I want this to become your strongest skill set.

# NEVER ANSWER THEIR QUESTIONS. WELL NOT UNTIL LATER ANYWAY. PART 2

Here is another reason you do not answer their questions as they ask them. Your answers may be wrong now, however your answers may be right later.

Asking the right questions can lead a customer to your answers. Answering the wrong questions will take you nowhere.

Let us take another look at the "color question".

A customer comes to you and asks "What colors does it come in?"

You answer with "They come in black or white."

They respond "Oh, I wanted red... I am going to look somewhere else."

Your answer and their response has just stopped the sale dead in the water. I will put the stoppage on you, the salesman, in this scenario. Don't do this. Don't answer like that. A question coming from a customer is never as black or white as it seems at face value. There is a lot more in the question than just yes, no, black or white.

It could be a loaded question to stop the sale and protect their money.

Your answer was wrong. So they used it to justify not buying. Again they are protecting the money.

Your answer was wrong. However they may have been open to a different answer. Here is a better response to this color question example:

Customer asks "what color does it come in?"

Your response "may I ask what color you are looking for, how do you see it in your mind?"

Customer answers "red."

Now at this point, don't answer with we only have black or white. Acknowledge their answer. Maybe with a nod of your head or a positive statement similar to "red is a nice color".

And I must point out here, don't answer with something like "red would be a nice color". Avoid the word "would" in this interaction. The word would can and will open up the client at this moment to questions that could and will derail the interaction. Instead follow up with another question to keep the conversation moving forward. For example:

You nod in agreement and ask "how are you looking to improve your ____ with this ____ ?"

Continue on with your questions. And continue questioning their questions to determine what it is they are really looking for. When you have gained enough insight into what they want. What they really want. You can then lead them to your "black or white" one which answers all their needs, so they can justify purchasing.

So remember. They said red, however they might be happy with black.

# SECTION 4: BASIC TECHNIQUES 2

Now that you have learned the client's name, are asking more questions instead of answering them, and are going to ask for the Close. Let's see if we can strengthen your foundational skills.

# TELL ME ABOUT.....

"**Tell Me About....**" What a great phrase. This is a great way to get the conversation started. **It is literally a command to start the client talking** and is very effective in helping you clarify what the client's questions actually are.

This is an expansion of Asking Questions Instead of Answering Them. By asking them to "Tell You About it", frees them to start talking. Then as they talk, you can pepper in some more questions. Guide them with just enough answers to move them forward. Here are a couple of suggestions or examples for you to start developing in your own area of sales.

"Tell me about your friend's…."

"Tell me what you saw at the…."

"Tell me about the upcoming event….."

"Tell me about the time that you….."

"Tell me about what …. were wearing."

"Tell me about what …. were driving."

"Tell me what would be the (perfect, worst, best)…."

"Tell me about your previous experience…."

If there is something you need to know about a customer or client? Are you wondering what they are thinking? Do you need to know how they plan to use it, how do they think it should operate, or what would be their ideal version? Find out what they are thinking and ask them to **tell you about it**.

# LEARN THEIR LANGUAGE.

When asking questions. Listen to the client. Take note of how they express themselves or refer to something.

Learn their "Language".

We are not talking about their spoken language, as in English or Chinese. But how they understand the topic and what words that they use to explain it.

When you start to understand what they mean by statement X. You can understand the solutions for X. You can help them to clarify what X really means or is. When the appropriate moment to educate arises you can help them to understand and talk about X.

Here is an example. In this case you work in an Electronics Store. A customer comes in and asks for an amplifier. But what amplifier? What do they mean? Is it for a Stereo System to listen to music? Is it for a Dolby Atoms Surround System to watch movies? Or both? Do they even know? This is where you, through questioning, Learn Their Language. Here would be a good place for a "Tell Me About …"

"Tell me. How do you plan to use….?"

"Tell me about the last time you…..?"

"What would you like to do with….?"

"What do you need it to do?"

Hopefully from their answers you will have an "Ah, I See" moment.

Now you can speak with them in their language and help them to learn a little of yours.

Do not try to teach them yours first though. You will just scare them away.

# SELL THEIR SERVICE.
# NOT YOUR SERVICE.

Here is yet another expansion of asking questions.

Are you starting to see how important it is to ask those questions?

When you are asking a customer or client questions to learn what has motivated them to come to your showroom, **Sell them the service that they want. Not the service you are offering.**

When you spend time questioning the client and picking up on their language. Learn to present the service or product you offer in their terms, their language, their needs. Use their language to build upon their desires. Use their language to help them justify the Close whenever possible.

Here are two examples to help you understand. Again, in this example you are working in an Electronics Store that sells Home Theater Systems.

A customer comes in for an "Amplifier". You learn that they want to watch movies with their family. They want to spend time with their family. That is what is important to them. So, don't sell them a "Dolby Atmos Surround Sound Processor". That is not their language, that is not their desire. Sell them a solution to bring their family together. Question them, educate them and guide them. Until you can connect in their mind that a "Dolby Atmos Surround Sound Processor" will bring them "Maximum Family Fun on Movie Night" stick with their Language.

In this second example your customer comes in and asks for "Dolby Atmos Surround Sound Processor". They are well educated in the technology already. They have a language and an understanding that supports the deepest technical aspects of a surround sound amplifier for watching movies. In this case you're not selling them the family experience. You are selling them the Dolby Atmos Surround Sound System with 9 channels with 150 watts each and two subwoofer outputs.

Sell them what they want. Sometimes it will be exactly what you are selling already. But if they want that family experience. Sell them the next level of family experience.

## TELL THEM THEIR STORY AGAIN AND AGAIN.

Through questioning the client, learning their language and what is motivating them, there will be a point where you start to develop a good understanding of what the client's desires are and how to relate those desires to the client. Turning your new understanding, to the helping of the client, in justifying Closing on those desires.

Tell a story that involves the client in using your goods or services. Tell them their story again and again. This goes hand in hand with asking questions like "What color do you see the ……….. as, in your living room?" Asking them what they want, how they see it, or plan to use it will reveal the true answers and reasons behind their wants and desires to you.

Now that you have the answers underlying their desires, it is time to deepen those desires and build their justifications. Tell them their story. Involve them in the story using the insights you have learned. Use their answers as key points in desire building stories to help them Close on those desires. Here are a couple ideas for you to think about.


"Think about how that ………….. would look in your living room. Imagine sitting down to enjoy that for an evening."

"Imagine spending a night watching a movie with your family on that screen. They would never want to go out again."


Keep weaving in the client's motivations into the stories that you tell. Every Close should involve the client in the story. The story should be one that they can relate to, and it should build desire helping them to Close on that desire.

They may be trying to create their own version of a story that they have seen on TV. They may buy fancy clothes, so that they can see themselves as a character from their favorite movies. They may be trying to create the perfect interior for their home. Tell them their stories. Have them live the experience in their own minds.

# TELL ME WHAT YOU HAVE LEARNED ALREADY.

Ask your client what they may have **already learned or what they may already know**. Use this when you are questioning a client, and try to do this early in the conversation. We are trying to get an idea of what they do or do not know about the product or service they are looking for. But more importantly we are trying to find out where they learned what they think they may know. Was it at another dealer, the internet, a friend, or do they already have previous experience?

"Is this your first ……? May I ask what you know so far?"

"Have you read the review about ……., in X Magazine?"

"Have you ever seen or heard a …….. before?"

"Tell me, have you ever …… ?"

"How do you find the available information online?". "Does it help?"

However do not ask questions that may cause the buyer to lie to you. You want them to feel like they can answer you honestly. So do not make them lie. For example don't ask about a competitor's pricing, if you find out they have been at another dealer already. This kind of question will cause them to lie to you. For now, just knowing they are shopping around helps.

If they have been at your competitors recently, be complementary and positive about your competitors. Try never to put them in a bad light. If the customer says something negative about their experience at a competitor, do not jump on it. Just say that is unfortunate. Remember it could be a trap.

Their answers will help you understand them more and help you to consider a direction to take further questioning. For example, they have been on internet forums, and you may need to clear up a few things for them.

And remember asking questions helps build rapport.

We just want to find out what they may know and where they learned it.

# CUSTOMER KEEPS MOVING THE TARGET AROUND.

When the customer keeps moving the target around or keeps talking about anything but the sale. You need to gently cut the thread and put the conversation back on target.

Every now and then you will run into a customer that comes in to talk about brand X. But they keep moving the conversation around to Y or Z or their car. This can be frustrating to deal with. Keep calm and don't let frustration get the better of you. Sometimes it will feel like the client is just there to talk. And maybe they are. However maybe they are just overwhelmed at the moment.

Try not to let them stray. It will be better for both of you to stay focused. It is ok for you to pull them back on track.

Now here is a caveat to this Idea. If in their continuous offshoots, you see an opening for a sale with a stronger Closing potential. It may be time to restart your questioning down the new thread. It is alright to ask them if the new thread is what they are really here for.

Remember, technically, you're not there to make Friends. You are here to help your client Close on their desire by helping them rationalize the sale. So don't let them ramble on.

# NEVER EVER SAY THE WORDS BUY OR COST.

"Would you like to Buy it?"

Or

"The cost of that is…."

Use the words "Buy" or "Cost", and you might as well get a needle and some nylon thread and help your client sow their wallet shut.

In sales, the words "Buy" or "Cost" have very negative connotations in the mind of a customer. To Buy is to Spend and spending money is in direct conflict with the rational mind's need to keep control of the wallet. And the "Cost" can be interpreted as "It will cost you". As the old expression goes "It will cost you an arm and a leg" has never been a good thing.

We need to speak with the client in the Positive and avoid the Negative. Here are a few examples of negatives vs positives.

Never say "Buy" or "To Buy". Instead use "Own" or "Ownership". To buy something just means spending money and it hurts to spend. To own something because of an exchange brings pride and joy.

Never say "It Costs" or "The Cost of". Use "Investment" or "Your Investment". When someone invests, they can expect a good return. As you are trying to Close them on their desires, their rational mind will see an Investment as a positive way to achieve their desire. As opposed to the irrational Costs of their desires.

Furthermore.

Never use the words "Price" or "Purchase". Because a Price or a Purchase will have a Cost that may be too high to justify. Again express yourself positively, use Ownership or Investment.

Finally.

Never use the word "Contract". Use "Agreement". Contracts are binding serious things. An Agreement has less serious connotations. It is a lot less stressful to "Write up an Agreement" between you and the client for their new investment, then it is to "Write up the Contract" and the binding cost of that contract.

However, since you need to ask the client to buy or purchase your goods to Close. Here are a few alternative phases for you to ask for the Close.


"Shall we write this up."

"Because you are here. Shall we write it up."

"Shall we write up the agreement."

"Is it time to take …… home."

"Invest in yourself. It's time to take it home."

"Where would you like it delivered?"

"You will feel the pride of ownership that comes from a modest Investment." "Shall we …."


So, remember to avoid the negative connotations of Buy or Cost. Install pride of ownership through a positive investment in their future.

# NEVER SAY "BUT". USE "HOWEVER".

This is a very good lesson to learn. Never use the word "BUT". Use "However". The word "But" is too strong and firm of a statement. "But" negates or cancels what was said before. Try saying it to yourself. Try this. See how it feels.

"That is very nice."... "But"

"That's your opinion."..."But"

Can you feel the jolting and halting effect that has? When you say "But" to your customer, it's the same as disagreeing or arguing with them outright. The word "But" diminishes, or even worse, disregards what has been said by the person you are talking with. Making it hard or almost impossible to have your client consider an alternative point. Instead use the word "However".

"That is very nice." "However"

"That's your opinion." "However"

"However, would you consider?"

"I like that." "However…"

Feel how the word "However", has a less aggressive edge to it. It can be used to offer up an option or an alternative without the momentum of the conversation coming to a halt.

Remember "But" is a Negative. "However", is a positive with possible options to consider.

Learn to replace but with however in your vocabulary. You will get people to listen.

# THERE ARE NO DUMB QUESTIONS.

What do you do when a client asks a really uninformed or dumb sounding question?

First, when asked, do not react as if they have asked the stupidest question you've heard today. And yes, it may be shockingly off track. **But do not react negatively or judgmentally in any way.** Keep your reaction to yourself. It cannot show on your face. Or you will lose them.

Second, ask questions to get to the heart of their question. They may be really misinformed about your products or services, they may have received bad advice and information from friends or the internet, and or they simply don't know, and don't know how to ask the question. Remember, questions are your friend. They will guide your interaction with the client. So slow down a little. Ask pertinent questions. Ask them directly if they understand. Guide them and get them on track towards acquiring their desires.

Now on the other hand, they may directly say "I have a dumb question". Your response here will be. **"There are no dumb questions".**

This is a fantastic opportunity to build rapport with the client. Responding with "there are no dumb questions" will have the effect of freeing the customer to open up to you. It will bring you closer to the client and provide more opportunity to ask them questions.

Sometimes the customer won't ask a question out of the fear of looking stupid. Their pride gets the better of them. In this case

with an unresponsive client who won't open up to you. Tell them directly.

"There are no dumb questions."

and

"Don't be afraid to ask."

It will help them to stop putting up barriers, and open them to be engaged with. Let them know that the more questions they ask the more you can help them.

## THE CLIENT MAY NOT KNOW WHAT THEY REALLY WANT, BECAUSE THEY DON'T KNOW WHAT'S REALLY OUT THERE.

Have you ever gone out to buy one thing and come back with another?

Maybe the client does not know what is really available. This is why we question a client. They may be looking for product X because they suddenly have developed a desire for X, however they may really be looking for XY.

Let's use a music system as an example. Your client comes to your showroom, because you sell audio equipment for home stereos and he wants to start listening to music again.

He tells you he was listening to music at a friend's house. The friend had a small portable speaker and thought very highly of it. And he thinks he wants something similar.

In your audio store you sell small portable speakers like his friend's piece. You also sell stereo systems that can range in price from five thousand dollars to a hundred thousand dollars or more with the performances to match.

With your help, through questions and demos. The client may come to learn what he really wants. Instead of the little portable, he could end up with much much more. Getting the music system he really wanted.

Before a client comes to you they may have something in mind, but truly don't understand what options are really available. Through questions and demonstrations, help them to learn, and come to understand the possibilities.

Here is something I want you to try. After proper questioning and demos, if I felt the client was truly ready to move beyond what they had originally come to me for. I would try a Test Close on them with their first ideas. By moving back to the original and trying a test Close on them, you will learn what they are thinking and where their head is at. You may learn that they are thinking about the new options, the ones that they learned about from you. This test Close will have the effect of helping them to solidify their desire and justify the move up to the higher quality offerings.

# LOW MIDDLE HIGH.

I feel like I shouldn't even have to mention this technique. But the old "Low Middle and High" as it is known can be a very effective sales method. The basic idea of this method is to offer a client a lower priced option, a middle priced option, and a higher priced option. The reason for the three options, often is to sell the middle option.

People have a built-in bias to move towards the safest choice. This bias is very hard to ignore or overcome. Look honestly at yourself and some of the decisions to purchase you have made, and you will see this in yourself. When offered the three choices of Low Middle or High. Most people will pick the middle choice. The Middle Choice is most often perceived as the safest. The middle choice gets them closer in performance to the higher priced choice without the higher price tag, and it provides far better performance and higher quality than the lower priced choice.

Choosing the middle option is also good for the customer's own sense of self worth. A customer won't feel like they are being too cheap, and better yet they will feel like they have gotten a good deal. They have made the right choice and won't feel like they spent too high a price for the product or service.

Let's apply the Low Middle High technique to what we are learning here.

You have learned to use questioning to guide a client towards their final desire. As you come to understand your client's motivations, start to build in your mind the Low Middle and High options. The Middle option being the one you would like to guide them towards.

You can use the Low and the High to help their rational brain to justify the Middle and ultimately satisfy their desires. This will help them to choose the right choice, moving them to acquire it and Close on these wants and desires.

# YOU NEVER GET MORE BY PAYING LESS. PART 1.

"You never get more by paying less". This is a great comment to use when confronted by the client's rational mind's inherent cheapness that is trying to protect the wallet.

You have a client. And through questioning you have determined what is the best solution for the client. The client may even agree with you, and they know already that this is the best solution for them. However, the client is protesting the price of your product or worse yet they have found some cheaply made version of what you are trying to help them to bring home.

Remember your duty. They are here trying to get help rationalizing the purchase they really want to make.

When this happens. It can be hard to defend the more expensive piece to an inexperienced customer with no prior knowledge of the product you are offering. All they may "know" is what they have learned online or from some "expert" who is no expert at all.

Try to resist the urge to defend your product at this moment. It will just weaken your position with the client. Instead of defending your product against this "cheaper" alternative. Hit them with this line.

"You never get more by paying less".

The client may protest. So calmly say it again.

"You never get more by paying less".

The client may ask you. "What do you mean?" or ask you to explain yourself. Now, you can defend your statement, without defending the product directly. Here is a good follow up that I hope you can mold to fit your personal style when offering your product or service.

"Let me explain what I mean by this."

"Give me just a moment to clarify my meaning."

"Say you have two products. One sells for $1000 and one sells for $3000."

"Both have similar performance on paper."

"However."

"The manufacturers that produce each product hired designers."

"In each case the manufacturer had a desired final selling price for their product."

Now look at the customer and make sure they are following you. Now continue.

"The designer working to come up with the $3000 dollar product will have a higher budget, a wider range of options, and more time to put into designing the product."

"Whereas the designer working on the $1000 dollar product will have a smaller budget, less options and less time to finish their design."

Now you can defend your higher priced product to the client against the cheaper model.

"It's because of these differences that our product performs at a much higher level with less chance of breakdown or failure."

# YOU NEVER GET MORE BY PAYING LESS. PART 2.

"Good things are not cheap and cheap things are seldom good."

This is a great response for you to use when you receive a price objection or the client is referencing a cheaper product.

When you receive the price complaint. Ignore the objection to price. It may just be a complaint. Often complaints are just complaints. Acknowledge it and move to delivering your response.

When you deliver a response like this, be wary of the client's mood and the tone of your conversation thus far.

For example, use it light heartedly when appropriate, or use it matter of factly when the client needs a justification to act on their desire. Stay aware of the situation and you will know the correct delivery.

Now to deal with the customer's cheaper product. Refer back to 'You Never Get More By Paying Less. Part 1'. Use its lesson to help you move past the less expensive version.

# I UNDERSTAND. CAN YOU SHARE WITH ME YOUR CONCERNS?

When you feel that the client has an objection or concern that they have not shared. Try asking them directly.

"Can you share with me your concerns?"

"I see something is bothering you. Please tell me…"

"Tell me, what are you thinking?"

You need to find out any objections so that you can deal with them. By now you know to ask questions. But, maybe you haven't asked the right one.

Getting them to express their concerns helps to build rapport, and helps you to find the information you need to lead the client to Close on their desires.

When you discover what is bothering them. You can decide then whether to address it. Or move on. It may be a genuine concern that you need to tackle now, or it could be just a complaint.

So if you think something is off. Tell them to tell you.

# DEALING WITH THE EXPERT. PART 1.

Some day you are going to have to deal with the client's "Expert". This Expert is usually a friend of theirs. This person can be your worst enemy or a great accomplice. This Expert your client is taking advice from has your client's ear and confidence. You will need to handle this so-called Expert with great care.

Sometimes the client's expert is genuinely there to help. If this is the case, count your blessings, as it is rarely the situation. Make them a friend, and they will be of tremendous use.

Generally though the Expert can be a giant pain. You will need to deal with this Expert and get them on your side. Getting them to actually be a help and not a hindrance can most often be very difficult to do.

They can crash the sale or be of great service to you and your client.

Your client will bring this Expert along to help make a decision because they supposedly know something about the products or service you are providing. But the problem is they may know nothing about your product. They know just enough to be dangerous. Or worse yet, what they "Know" is dead wrong.

These Experts aren't paying for the product and often give advice from the perspective of their own wallets. Often, you will feel as if they are only there just to tank the sale. You may even get the feeling they are jealous of your client and are there just to put up roadblocks to stop the Close.

As you can see. Dealing with the Expert can be tricky. Sometimes they can be quite adversarial and will seem to disagree with you, just to disagree with you.

When you are dealing with this Expert, an old Dale Carnege strategy comes in very handy. Agree with them. Agree with the Expert right away.

"I agree."

"You're right about that."

"Isn't that the truth."

By agreeing, you remove conflict. Without conflict between you and the Expert, you can then start to build rapport. When you agree with the Expert, you can come together on common ground, then on common ground you can come to an understanding. With this understanding they can be brought on board to actually help as you introduce the client to the right solutions.

As you proceed, include the Expert in the discussion. Learn their name and use it often. As often as you would use the client's. Treat the Expert as the co-client. Think of the two of them as a client with two minds, and you are trying to get the two minds to come together on the same track.

As you include the Expert in the discussion. Ask them questions. In this situation you may be asking the client the question. But it is clearly aimed at the Expert. You want to know what they think or what they think they know. What are their opinions? You need to discover what the Expert's opinions are, as at the moment they are technically the client's opinions.

Ask the Expert what they think. Get them to tell their story. As they probably love the sound of their own voice and want to show off their "knowledge". Believe me they will tell you. They want to tell.

If you can get a firm grasp on the Expert's knowledge and

opinions you can steer your questions and demos to avoid conflict with the Expert.

For example, your product has X, Y, and Z attributes. Knowing the Expert doesn't care for X focus on Y and Z in your demo. Emphasize the superior performance of your products Y and Z attributes.

Now you know that the Expert will have to give their opinion. So when they tell you something like, they think that W is better than X. Don't argue. It's a trap. Remember the Expert's knack for sabotage. You weren't even talking about W at all. They are just trying to show off to your client. So stop them. Stop them by agreeing with them. Let them know that you would also actually prefer W. After you make peace. You can get back on track by letting everyone involved know that even though you agree, however, for Y and Z to achieve the performance you have demonstrated in your product, W Y and Z, cannot match the overall performance of X Y and Z. You will have not embarrassed the Expert and believe me the client is listening to you.

It will help you to ask the client what he thinks about the Expert's experience. Be tactful, but you need to learn this bit of information. It will tell you why the Expert is with the client. Does the Expert use a product or service similar to yours. How does this experience make the client feel? So as you go on with questioning, learning their co-language and their stories. You can try to meld the two minds until the expert fades away.

So to summarize. Include the Expert at first and don't shun them. Do not argue with him. Agree with them at first. Learn their name and use it often. As you learn a few things. It will become easier to use their "expertise" in your favour. Then you can ask questions that the Expert will answer with enthusiasm. Use your new ally to confirm what you are trying to teach the client.

# DEALING WITH THE EXPERT. PART 2.

In the last section we were successful in getting the Expert on our side. Unfortunately this is not always possible and the Expert will often remain adversarial throughout your time together with the client. There will come a moment when and where you will need to be more aggressive in dealing with the Expert. This will have to be done with some delicacy and perhaps some humor. Here are a couple things you could ask the Expert.

"Will you be chipping in?"

"Will you be helping with payment for all or a part of the ……..?"

Of Course the answer is no.

Don't drop this until later in your time with the client. This will start the flushing of the Expert from the sale as they have no financial stake in the sale. It will lessen the Expert's influence as it is the client's opinion that counts, and the client has the final say. This will help strengthen the client's position and move them closer to a Close of the sale. Remember they came to you, because you have what they developed a desire for.

They may have brought their Expert along. They don't have to agree with them.

# DEALING WITH THE EXPERT. PART 3.

This next bit of advice is very dangerous. Do not attempt until you know the Expert is absolutely going to tank your sale, and you have no other choice. Maybe just read the next part out of curiosity.

When the Expert has it in their mind to continuously divert, argue and is genuinely trying to crash the sale. You can try to flush them and their so-called expertise with this. However if you try this, you have to be confident in yourself and your expertise. This is a last ditch move. But the Expert is just out to stop the sale. So try this.

In a commanding voice say.

"Hey"

Get eye contact. Then proceed with

"Everyone in the room raise, your hand that has installed or sold over a hundred ………." (Use an example related to your business.)

"Everyone, raise their hand that has over … years of experience. And has personally worked with … products."

No one is going to raise their hand.

It will probably be dead silent at this moment.

Now raise your own hand. And say.

"I just wanted to know who I am dealing with."

When you get the answer you expected. That no one in the room but you has your experience. You then say with confidence and strong eye contact.

"This is why you have come here."

"I have done …… 100 plus times."

"I do have the years of experience."

"That's why I am here."

"To give you that experience."

This is a very dangerous technique for dealing with the "Expert" or even the reluctant client who simply refuses to believe in your expertise. Remember, because you are a salesperson, often you will be perceived as just trying to take their money. It's an effective way to reestablish your role as the actual expert in the room. But it's like using a sledge hammer to do it.

I have used it effectively. But very very sparingly. In today's economy there is so much info out there in the world and on the internet that clients can and will become confused, and confused with your role as an expert consultant. Sometimes you just have to bring things to a stop, to start them up again in the right direction.

In time when you have become more versed in sales techniques and are more comfortable in your role. The Raise your Hand can be used with humor to break down barriers with a nervous closed off customer and establish the customer consultant relationship in a fun and unexpected way.

# NEVER USE THE PHRASES "TO BE HONEST WITH YOU" OR "TRUST ME".

Never say to a customer or client "Trust me" or "To be honest with". Well. Not until you know without a doubt that they do believe you and they do trust you. And even then try to avoid their use. When trying to gain someone's trust, these words can and will destroy any developing connection you have created in a client relationship.

Remember, in this relationship you are a salesperson. As a salesperson you are most often perceived as a predator out to take someone's money. Using the words "trust me", simply means you are lying, or will lie when it suits you. This is a very hard stigma to get around. This stigma is the reason why we spend such great effort to build good rapport with those we are trying to do business with.

"To be honest with you". The second worst thing you can say in this category. Again it's another stigma of being in sales, most customers will perceive salespeople as dishonest. When they hear you say "To be honest with you", they may ask themselves questions along the lines of "Why are you being honest now, were you not honest earlier?" "Does this mean you can be deceitful, or untruthful? "

Be Careful.

I will not tell a customer to trust me. Unless I know for sure how something is going to happen. For example, the client asks, "can it be here on Monday?" If I know for an absolute fact it will. I will say trust me. When it does arrive on Monday your trust level will soar. If it does not show up. Regaining any trust you had with the client can be a daunting struggle.

Here is some further advice and a warning. Never tell a customer "Trust me" or "To be Honest with you" when talking about your product or service performance and functions. This is a very dangerous thing to do. If they ask you a direct question, they may be unsure that your product or service will perform as stated. To get the sale, you will be tempted to tell them to trust you, but if there is even the slightest deviance to what you told them, things can and will sour very quickly. There could be attempts to return your product and get their money back. There could even be bad reviews with your name on it. Remember that logical side of their brain that protects the wallet. It will be delighted to jump on your lie, and it will be more than happy to get the money back, even if it means ruining you to do it. They will never trust you again.

Your customer wants to be able to trust you. Use trust carefully. Better to prove yourself as trustful. Earn it. When you have it. The trust will be powerful.

# WHEN THEY ALREADY KNOW WHAT THEY WANT.

When a client walks in and they know exactly what they want. Just sell it to them. When they know what they want, just ask them what color they want. Be of good service. And move on.

In this section. I want to help you with a particularly troublesome character. This is kind of a warning. This "well researched" customer that knows what they want can come off as off putting and rude. They probably have developed an opinion, and it won't be a good one, of you as a salesperson before even having met you. To them, you are simply in the way of purchasing the product.

They often come in HOT and can be tricky to deal with. Closed off, easily offended, and they do not want your options or opinions. They are the most protective customers of their money. Even asking what color they are looking for can be dangerous. Try to just give them what they want and move on for now.

That is until you have achieved a higher understanding of client interactions.

However, no one is impenetrable. Move with caution. As your skills grow, they will become easier to deal with. Wait for opportunities to appear. When they do, ask clarifying questions that they can answer, so the answers are theirs not yours.

# SOMETIMES CUSTOMERS JUST SUCK.

Sometimes no matter what you do, a customer just sucks and will never be a Client.

Now you will have to follow your gut on this. And it will take time to develop a good sixth sense about these clients. In time you will come to learn who the time wasters are. They are just there to take your time and knowledge only to go somewhere else with it. Distracting you from real opportunities with other potential clients. Or even worse they will buy it, but you know they are going to try to return it. I recommend that you do your best to clear them.

Be polite, don't be rude, and move on to the next client.

Early in your career this will be difficult. It will be difficult to ignore that piece of you that will see the opportunity, even if it is a remote one, to earn money. That drive to succeed can be hard to overcome in these situations. However, earning money from this kind of customer is too painful and can distract you from other more prosperous opportunities.

Here is something to help you in this situation. You can always "Pass on this opportunity."

Again, be very polite, don't be rude and say something like:

"Thank you, however I will have to pass on this opportunity"

"I don't think I can be of service at this moment. I will have to pass on this opportunity."

"Thank you for the opportunity, but I will have to pass at this time."

See how effective that is. Since you are not being rude there is nothing for them to say or complain about.

Now you are free to assist others that you can assist in purchasing their wants and desires.

# INTENSIFY THE DESIRE TO BUY.

As we finish off with the basic techniques. Remember, everything you have learned so far and everything to come in the following sections is to intensify the clients Desire to Buy and justify the sale.

Use what you have learned here already. Get started right away. What you have learned up till this point will be a great foundation for you to rely on when engaging a client. Re-read the sections over and over. Learn these lessons. Make them your own, so you can develop your style.

Remember to lean on your questioning to get to the heart of the client's desire. Help them to justify the desire. And of course ask for the sale.

# SECTION 5: ADVANCED TECHNIQUES

Here we will explore techniques of a deeper, more advanced nature. Further developing your skills. Helping you, to help the client, so both of you can receive the benefits of the exchange through the Closing of their desire.

# WHAT IS THE ADVANCED SECRET TECHNIQUE?

Here is the advanced secret technique. ASK FOR THE CLOSE. Again, ask for the dam Close. This drives me furious. In myself and in others. Everyone will have a moment where they freeze on this. Say you are selling something outrageously expensive. I mean expensive. You have made all your presentations. You are talking their sales language. You know that this is what they want. They have told you their story. You are selling them their version of your service. Now help them. Ask for the Close. Have courage.

Now onto some next level techniques.

# HOW TO SAY HELLO.

This is one of the most important moments in a sale. The initial contact with a potential new client.

This has to be said here. Not everyone likes a salesperson. There are many stereotypes that persist concerning our profession. We have to deal with the fallout of unethical and greedy behavior demonstrated by those in sales without good moral character.

So the very act of saying hello to a customer can often be seen as adversarial. We need to be conscious of this. The following techniques will help you to address this successfully.

I feel the following are probably the most important lessons in this manual. In the next six sections we will discuss the word Hello. The act of saying hello. And how to deal with this encounter. We want to remove the chance of failure at first contact.

# HELLO PART 1: TO SAY HELLO. OR NOT TO SAY HELLO. THAT IS THE QUESTION.

How do you say hello and not destroy your first contact with a potential client? As you must get past this point of contact. Everyone of us has to deal with this sometimes painful encounter. The subject of how to say "Hello" could be a book by itself.

Let us first start with the client's point of view. I want you to see this from their perspective.

When you enter a store, and the salespeople are jumping all over you to get that hello in. What is your first thought? It's probably "get away from me". If not something harsher.

Remember until you break down the barriers and build rapport with a potential new client, they will most likely see you as a "salesman", with all of its negative connotations, someone that is just trying to take their money.

And to be kind to the salespeople coming at you as you enter a store. It's probably not their fault. They most likely have been instructed to aggressively say hello. They probably have some sales manager on them about it and are being watched. They probably get scolded for not saying hello emphatically. It is an old, outmoded management practice.

And the feelings clients have of possibly being taken advantage of is getting worse, as more people shop online and have fewer public interactions on a showroom floor. So, we must get past this moment. We must break down the barriers.

My hope here is that I can help you to "say hello" to a customer without destroying the opportunity to make a sale before you even get a chance to try.

**A customer enters your showroom.**

The first thing you should do is let them breathe for a second. Don't just jump all over them. Let them take in their new surroundings and adjust for a moment.

Their brains are taking in a lot of information quickly. It can be overwhelming.

They are probably feeling a little bit of excitement and fear. They are excited about satisfying a desire and fearful that they have to pay for it. If you jump on them too early the excitement and fear will turn into a retreat to safety. The worst being they make an excuse and just leave. If they stay their guard will be up and you will have a much longer, harder road ahead trying to build rapport and break down their barriers.

**The first person who talks loses.**

This may seem a little hard edged, however it is true.

You talk first. They retreat.

They talk first. You can advance.

Try not to be the first person to talk in this initial encounter. Don't ignore clients as they enter your showroom. Acknowledge them with a polite nod or a wave of your hand. It is ok to let them see that you know they are there. Try to be open and positive.

Wait to approach or to be approached. When they say hello, you now have permission to greet them formally and start the process of Closing them on their desires.

# HELLO PART 2: HELLO THROUGH GEOGRAPHY.

A great way to get the customer to engage you first, is to use the geography of your showroom to your advantage.

Use the showroom floor space to allow a customer to approach you. Position yourself in the room where they can see you, but you pose no threat.

What gets a lot of salespeople shot down, is a sales guy waiting right by the front door like a Walmart greeter.

**Don't do this.** When a customer comes in the front door and you hit them with a hello and a smile right away. You haven't even given them a chance to look around and take a breath.

Bam!

Hello!

And that is it. You are now the enemy.

A very powerful way to overcome this is through location. For example, In a smaller showroom position your desk or a customer counter at the back of the room. Don't hide back there. A customer must be able to see you. A showroom arranged in this way will bring a customer to your location. Forcing them to make the first move.

As they enter the room you can look up. You can even nod in their direction giving them permission to approach. Don't be standoffish. Be open. Don't lose a chance for engagement by being seen as arrogant.

What is nice about letting them approach you, is that you might be *working on something*. This gives you a chance to pause. Allowing them time to compose themselves and ready themselves to ask their questions. Which will often start with "hello can you help me?" Now that they have initiated the contact. You can say hello and get to work.

In a larger showroom it is the same idea. You may be positioned at or near the middle of the room. Giving the customer a bit of space and allowing the customer a moment to themselves before approaching you. Again, you must be seen, and have an open approachable air about you. And a simple nod in their direction will suffice.

To summarize. Don't talk first. Be approachable. Let them approach and initiate contact.

# HELLO PART 3: WHAT'S GOT YOU STOPPING BY?

Of course, you cannot always wait for the customer to talk first.

So let's defeat the negative impact of the "Hello".

The mind set here is to have customers feel safe, even if you do have to talk first. Here is a cheat code to defeat the negative effects that the "Hello" can have. So if you have to talk first, instead of "hello" try.

"What's got you stopping by today?"

Or if you have to include a hello to get their attention, combine the two.

"Hello". "What's got you stopping by?"

The reason this has such a powerful and calming effect on the customer's mind, is that if they are just stopping by, then they aren't actually shopping. And if they aren't shopping, then they are just taking a look around. There is no harm in just taking a look. No harm at all. They don't have to be afraid of the big bad salesman. Their money is safe.

See how simple that is.

With this simple phrase "What's got you stopping by?", you have given them the permission they need to let their guard down, neutralizing the inevitable tension caused by saying hello to a customer that enters a store. When a potential client enters your showroom they often bring a lot of tension with them. They will see themselves as a mark. In their mind they literally brought you the kill. You can get them off of this thought process by simply asking them "What has got you stopping by?".

Deliver this line right and you will see the tension drop from their shoulders.

Here is a warning. "What's got you stopping by?" works, as it is non committal. Don't turn it into a question requiring an answer. For example "What are you here for?" or "What are you looking for?". A question like one of these requires commitment. You will find what they are here for later. Let's break down their barriers, not help them build them.

# HELLO PART 4: DOING A LITTLE RESEARCH?

Here is another version of the "What's got you stopping by?" technique. Say to a customer.

"Doing a little research?"

Or

"Stopping by to do a little research?"

With this version, a customer has not come to your store to purchase something, they are just simply doing a little research. Their money's safe, and the logical side of their brain is free to let down its guard a little. Research is free and safe.

With this short comment, you have given them safety. Believe me they will appreciate it.

Now it's a little safer to ask them some questions. Because you may be able to help them research their questions.

After giving them a safe reason to be in your store, give them a moment to look around and take in their surroundings. Then let them know.

"If you have any questions let me know."  "I am here to help."

They will have questions.

# HELLO PART 5: THE SECRETARY INTRODUCTION.

This one is called the **Secretary Introduction.** As the use of a secretary or member of a team whose job it is to greet is traditionally the secretaries job.

The use of a secretary or greeter is one of the safest ways for people in sales to meet new potential clients. As it deflects the dreaded tension of meeting a new potential client away from the salesperson through the use of an intermediary.

The reason it works is that people know and generally accept that a greeting from a secretary is safe. It is in fact their job. And the fact that they aren't in sales makes them approachable and safe to converse with.

Think about meeting someone for the first time. You don't know them and they don't know you. Imagine the nerves and anxiety you may have if you were to approach them for the first time. Both sides not knowing or quite trusting the other. Now picture how much easier it feels meeting someone new if you are introduced to them through a common acquaintance.

The common acquaintance here being the Secretary.

This is why the Secretary Introduction works so well in your favor. It separates you , the salesperson, from the initial hello.

And the best part is you are being asked to introduce yourself. And since you didn't start the engagement with the customer hopefully you can start the meeting in a positive and productive manner.

It negates the initial conflict of sales vs customer.

If you don't have a secretary or a greeter, I recommend working out an arrangement with another member or members of your salesforce. Take turns being the greeter and throwing yourself upon the spear of that initial "Hello".

With some practice this will become a very powerful tool.

# HELLO PART 6: THE FEINT.

So years ago, I worked in a place that had one of those managers that really jumped on you to say hello to people right as they came into the store. They just didn't know or accept the negative effects such aggressive technique had on people. They were just relying on older doctrine that they were taught.

Here I was caught between knowing how customers could/would react and the manager's commandments.

Out of the necessity of my situation came a great technique for dealing with this. I call it **The Feint**.

It's a physical way to attract the customer's attention. To lure them. To focus their mind and draw them towards you.

The name of this technique comes from a time I spent learning karate. The instructors used to teach us how to draw out an opponent by using our mind and body so that we could strike. We would use a **Feint** to draw the opponent in.

Let's see if I can explain how to perform and use **The Feint** successfully.

When a customer comes on to your showroom floor. You should stand in a spot that the customer will have to pass by you. But not so close as to block their path. Be visibly alert to their presence but not overbearing. If you can, leave a little space for them to escape to.

Because in this example we have to say hello to people as they enter the store, stay neutral and as peacefully as possible, say hello. This is the key moment. When they say hello back. And things could already be changing in their minds for the worse. You have to draw them out. This is when you use **The Feint**.

When they say hello back or just nod towards you. Make your move.

It's a subtle motion with your body that begins with a pulling away with your body. A slight turn. As if you are going to leave. Pulling away as if you were dragging a fishing lure behind you. They will reflexively reach out to you with both body and mind. The movement of your passive withdrawal will force their subconscious mind to race towards you.

Now even though you had to open first with a greeting. By pulling away they have reached out to you. Now you can engage on your terms.

I found this to be a fantastic technique that works on even the grumpiest of customers. It's a great feeling when they open up with a "Can you help me?" question. If I would have asked them the question first they would have pulled away immediately.

A warning here. This can backfire if not performed confidently and smoothly. So practice it as much as you can on your friends and coworkers.

This is a powerful tool that can be engaged in many more situations than the sales floor. Get good at it. Use it.

# SAYING HELLO IN THE OUTSIDE WORLD.

If you catch their eye, go say hi.

When you find yourself outside of the showroom, and a potential new client appears, the rules of engagement change.

Outside of the showroom, follow the **Three Second Rule**.

In this situation do the opposite of what you have learned so far. In this encounter you only have three seconds to act.

In social settings such as a conference, trade show, bar or golf club you will often see a potential client or simply someone that you would like to introduce yourself to. When the opportunity presents itself, or you catch their eye. **Go right to them**. You could be right next to them at the bar or across the entire room. When you do catch their eye. Move. You have three seconds. If you wait any longer you will come across as weak. Move before you lose your nerves. Go right up and say hello. In this setting it is a good thing to be overly friendly. In the store you will scare them away but here you will meet new and interesting people and find new opportunities.

Start with hello. Ask them their name, learn it, and use it often. Remember people love to hear their own name. If you need an opening line. Start with, "what has you coming to an event like this"(a version of the what's got you stopping by technique). Go with the listening approach. Ask questions about them. Again and again. You will know what to say if you know what their name and enjoyments are.

# SMILING.

"Smile, it's the key that fits the lock in everybody's heart."

I still don't believe I have to add this section, but often new salespeople need to learn this and the seasoned pro needs to relearn it.

Here are some notes for you on smiling.

Simply. Smiling is a wonderful way to build relationships with people. If you're not a person who smiles automatically and naturally, then learn to smile.

Because a genuine smile is easy for a customer to read, they will learn to trust you and feel safe with you. But also, it's just as easy to put a customer off if your smile is not very genuine or sly.

If you are a natural smiler. Feel blessed. It's a gift. If you don't naturally smile with ease, learn to smile. You can learn to smile by just walking around in your daily life, trying to smile all the time. And I mean all the time. When you are walking, shopping, talking on the phone, or anything you may be doing. Eventually you will learn to smile, and it'll become a natural reflex, and you won't have to practice, you'll just be smiling.

Smile. It's easy. Well they say that anyway. Of course you should smile while interacting with a client. But also. Don't overdo it. A non genuine smile will bury you. Customers can see a fake smile and will read you as fake. You probably have run into this smile before in your own life. It's very off putting. To me it feels like the person smiles with evil intent. Like they want to take something from me. Or advance themselves at my cost. I will want to separate myself from them immediately. So smile but be careful to not over do it. It would be better to not smile and look concerned with a customer's well being, than to have a fake disingenuous smile.

Now what do you do if you have a Resting Bitch Face? Well it's time to practice and develop a real and genuine smile. This advice comes from a real personal experience. The first time I realized I needed to work on my smile, was a real shock for me.

I like to think of myself as a genuine and easy going guy. But I guess I have a **Resting Bitch Face** sometimes. I discovered this when I was deeply following a person's story once sometime ago. And I was intently following their every word. Well, to my surprise, at one point they asked me "Do you even care what I am saying right now?". I tell you now, I was shocked. It turns out I had the coldest resting bitch face on the planet. I was genuinely interested in their story and felt deeply sorry.

Well. Since then, I have worked to let a person know they are interesting to me. So taking the news to heart, and not letting it affect my ego. I started to practice my smile. So, I am telling you to practice your smile. Practice all the time. It will genuinely change your attitude. Smiles are infectious. Like the saying goes, smile and the world smiles with you.

However, here's some almost contradictory advice when it comes to your smile. Don't just give it away to everyone. A neutral face that turns into a smile while making introductions, is a very powerful gesture. You could almost think of it as a half smile. That way when you turn it on to full after learning a new client's name. It will come across as more genuine and be infectious.

Half smiling while on duty is a good move. It doesn't cut you off from potential clients and helps to deliver the real thing.

When I greet a client. I do like to use the half smile followed by a full friendly smile. That way I feel the chance of rejection or "I am just looking around" diminishes.

So in your day to day life. Smile. Smile a lot. And if you are like me, you will need to train. But it will pay off. Now when I am out and about anywhere, it's easy for me to throw a smile to a passerby that will receive a great smile in return.

# DROP THE FAKE ENTHUSIASM.

Nothing bugs me more than fake, forced, canned enthusiasm. It's a sale killer.

You may have come across people in your own life where something is off about them, and you can tell they aren't being genuine with you. When confronted with this you probably had the desire to pull away and to distance yourself from them.

If you're not real with a potential client, you can and will kill your sale.

But what if you aren't actually that enthusiastic about what you are selling? Then you really only have two choices. Sell something else, which might not be an option, or figure out what excites you about the products or services you are representing and latch onto those points. Get excited.

What do you think? What can you come up with? Is it the quality of the product, is it what the product can do, is it better than the competition, or is it just the financial gain from Closing a sale on the product?

If you find yourself getting excited about the product after taking a deeper look. Great. Go with it.

If you said to yourself "it's just about the money", good, at least you are being honest. Here is some advice for you to develop real enthusiasm.

Learn to attach the chance of financial gain to the good points of the product or service you offer. See the good points you come up with as the reason you will make the sale. Get excited that the quality, the things it can do, and the fact it's better than the competition will benefit you financially. See every good point as a chance to earn, then you will develop real enthusiasm to help your clients Close on their desires.

Clients will appreciate talking to a real human being. Be genuine. Be real. You will go far.

# PEOPLE LOVE TO HEAR THEMSELVES TALK.

No really, they really do.

People love to hear themselves talk. They really do. They are the most reasonable person they know and generally agree with everything that they say.

So knowing that, we need to get them to talk. To tell their story. This is an expansion of asking them questions. When they have a story to tell. Let them tell you. If they won't tell their story, keep asking the questions that will get them to open up and start telling their story. In the telling of their story, their true desires will be revealed.

When they talk you will learn things like, how did they come to this conclusion, have they seen the product or service before, how did it affect them, and what made them want to repeat that experience?

When they tell their story they not only reveal to you what their wants and needs are, they will also strengthen their own desires at the same time.

When they tell their story you can pick up on their Language. What do they mean when they reference something? As they tell their story it will become easier to understand them.

Through stories you may come to see them as a buyer even though at first they did not appear to be one. Or, maybe they will reveal themselves to be just a time waster. With this insight you can then politely move on. Maybe you find out that the work you are putting into today could pay off tomorrow. Through their stories there is a lot to learn.

So don't waste time telling your story. It's probably only interesting to you. And will probably sound like you are just trying to sell something.

Remember the more that you can get them to say the more you can learn. The better you will be able to help them Close on the product or service they yearn for. And by helping them, you help yourself, your family, your company.

# ALWAYS BE CLOSING. PART 1.

A B C. Always be Closing. I am sure you have heard this expression before. Maybe in a movie or from a colleague? When we use the phrase **Always Be Closing** in relation to personal one on one selling we are talking about building the need in your customer to purchase with every one of your questions and desire building statements.

And to be clear here. When we say Always Be Closing, ***Anything and Everything*** you say to the customer or ask the customer is intended to lead them to saying yes both in their mind and out loud.

This section isn't so much a lesson on how to Close but the mentality I want you to develop. This is essentially the core of every lesson you have been presented so far. Use this mental state of Always Be Closing as the reason you ask questions or present a client with their truths.

I waited until now to present this as I wanted you to develop some essential skills and understandings first. This is the bedrock upon which the previous lessons stand.

So take those lessons and start really thinking about how you converse with a potential client.

# ALWAYS BE CLOSING. PART 2.

No wasted words.

Don't waste time with idle chit chat.

Close them by asking the right questions.

When you ask a question, Close them by putting the object of their desire into action in their mind.

When they ask a question, ask them the question right back, Closing them by putting the object of their desires into action in their mind.

Close them by trying test Closes.

Close them by telling them to see and hear things in their minds' eye. If they can see it in their mind it becomes real to them. Imaginations are quick.

Don't waste your words, guide them with your questions towards the Close.

Building their desire as you go.

So to sum it up. ALWAYS BE CLOSING. Everything you say and do should lead to a Close. If you do it right, when it's time to ask them "Shall we write it up?", they may beat you to it. And ask you to write it up.

# WHY WOULD YOU BUY THAT?

"Why are you looking for this at this time?"

"Why do you need it?"

"What's your reason for wanting our service?"

"Tell me why this one is the right choice."

Asking a customer or client these kinds of questions can be a very effective way to move them closer to a Close.

Instead of continuing to sell them on the product or service you offer, directly ask them why they want it. This can be very powerful. As they will be selling themselves when they tell you the reasons they are interested in making this purchase.

It's better for someone to come up with their own conclusions than to suggest the conclusion.

Getting a client to come up with their own conclusion is one of the best desires building tools you have. It helps them to justify the purchase by having them think about the reasons, then say them out loud.

In the process of questioning a client you will be leading them with your desire building questions, and strengthening their desires along the way. If in that process you can get the client to come to their own conclusion about what they need, what they want, and then have them tell you all about it. The idea becomes theirs. You may have been leading them there the whole way. But when it's their idea. It's not your idea. It's their decision. Their choice. It will be a lot easier to move them to the final Close and ask for the sale.

Some caution here is advisable. I would not recommend this direct of a question to be used too early in a negotiation. Wait a bit. Start with questioning them a bit about their needs first. Build a little desire in their mind with Closing statements that have them using the product or service in their head. Learn all you can about their wants and needs. Then when you are fairly certain of what they will say, drop this question on them. It will have a great effect on their desire as they list all the reasons to go ahead with the sale. I mean who better to sell them, then for them to sell themselves.

# NEVER DIRECTLY SAY THAT YOU ARE BETTER THAN THE COMPETITION.

It is up to you to teach and not tell the customer why you are better.

Telling a customer you are better than your competition can have a negative outcome for you. One way being that it sounds like bragging, and often people are put off by bragging. Another is that it may come off as a simple lie. People don't like liars. And finally your customer may disagree with you. And with that disagreement, you have created a situation where it's you versus the customer. Not a good situation. All of these situations can be recovered from, but it takes some tact on your part to smooth the tension between you. Better to just avoid it.

It is better to show some appreciation for your competitors' good points. I might say that "I am a big fan of that product and I do like what they are doing with it." Not shying away from the competition puts you on an even scale with the competition. Allowing you to have the client learn why your products or services more precisely fit their needs.

# DIRECTLY TELL THEM YOU ARE BETTER THAN THE COMPETITION.

I know this goes against what I just told you to do. But sometimes you will simply have to state that you are better than the competition.

I find that sometimes the customer just needs to hear it said. The caveat here being that they already believe it themselves. You are just confirming their belief. With proper questioning on your part you will know this, and know when to say it.

More commonly though, and this is directly related to the internet, a customer will come to you with a product that on paper may share similar aspects to your product. Because of the information and opinions that a customer will run into on the net, things can become murky, leaving the customer to have a hard time telling the difference between quality product and inferior imitators.

Here is a very real world example. Let's say you are offering high end solutions with unparalleled craftsmanship. Your product also comes with a premium price tag. Your customer tells you about a cheaper product that on paper has the same specifications, and furthermore so called "Experts" on the internet confirm this comparison. Your product has developed its reputation through years of quality output and dedication to never wavering from their practice of producing only the best. Gaining their reputation through word of mouth, with almost zero marketing budget, choosing to use their finances to produce the finest products available. The competitor on the other hand spends all of their finances on advertising and pays for reviews. The competition also uses low budget components to build their lower priced products.

Point out these comparisons and facts about yours and the competitor's products. Then tell the customer directly and bluntly that you are better than the competition.

# IF THE CLIENT ACTUALLY THOUGHT THE COMPETITION WAS BETTER THEY WOULD'VE ALREADY GONE WITH THEM.

Remember this. Keep this fact in the back of your mind. Stand on this foundation to keep your courage and spirits up when dealing with difficult clients and customers.

Use this bit of knowledge to see past what a customer is telling you during negotiations.

# I DON'T KNOW. PART 2.

If you don't know the answer, don't be afraid, use "I don't know" as a way to Close the client.

"I don't know…let's find out together."

Not knowing the answer to a customer's question can be scary. You get this feeling that because I don't know the answer, the customer will leave to find someone else who does.

Do not fear the question you can't answer. It is really an opportunity.

An opportunity to learn what your customer is thinking.

An opportunity to build rapport with your customer.

An opportunity to strengthen the customer's desire and move them towards the Close.

If they ask a question and you don't know the answer, tell them you don't know the answer. Let them know that this is a great question, and that you also would like to know the answer. At this moment say:

"Well that is a good question, I would also like to know that answer is, let's see if we can learn the answer to this together."

Now take them to where the answer is. It may be to sit down and check a computer together, look through a manual together, or even ask someone in your organization who might be an expert to explain it to you and the customer together.

Take the time to learn the answer together.

This is an easy and effective way to establish trust.

Important note here. Don't run off by yourself to get the answer. Do it together.

Yes it is great to have all the answers in your head. But sometimes, it's better to help the client *learn the answer together*.

# DO NOT ARGUE.

Do not argue with a customer or client. It will get you nowhere. Arguing is probably the best way to terminate any chance of a sale.

You will never get a person to change their mind in an argument. People will usually put up fences and defend their position in an argument. You will never be able to force someone to change their mind in a conflict of ideas.

So if you see an argument coming. Instead of arguing try one of these.

"I might be wrong."

"I see what you are saying."

Or simply, just agree with them.

Remove the conflict, and they will lower their defences.

Once you have acknowledged their point and found common ground in agreement, you will be in a much better position to help them to come to a new point of view, based on new learned facts. Facts they learn from you.

So to recap. Agree first, this will diffuse the situation. Then find out what their true belief is. Come to common ground. Let them know you understand their point of view. Then, when there is peace, introduce new ideas and help them to see a new point of view and come to a better mutual understanding.

Remember, in this situation do not use the word "but" as you will disregard everything they have said, and possibly reignite an argument. Always use "however", it will acknowledge their point of view and allow you to introduce new points to the conversation.

# COMPLAINTS. SOMETIMES, IT'S JUST A COMPLAINT. GET OVER IT AND MOVE ON.

Customer complaints can be scary to deal with. However, dealing with a customer complaint is not about dealing with their complaint. It's about dealing with you.

It's learning to master your emotional response.

Dealing with the complaints and objections a customer may pose while engaging with them during the sales process is one of the most important skills you need to learn and refine.

We need you to learn to not react emotionally to a complaint. Stay calm and see the complaint for what it really is.

Complaints are good.

Complaints tell you things. They can lead you in the right direction.

Most importantly the complaint means they want it. They really do. Their rational mind just needs to come to grips with the cost it will have on their wallet.

Sometimes complaints are just complaints. So I don't want you to get hung up on them anymore. I really want you to learn to push past them. Control your response and keep a calm demeanor. Almost ignoring the complaint. But don't really ignore them as they may be a key towards the right product or a way to uncover a missing piece of info you need.

Let's take a look at three examples of how to deal with a complaint.

Example one. A customer may say to you.

"It's expensive" or "it's too expensive ".

Don't react, just agree.

"Yes, I agree." or "Yes, it's a bigger investment".

See how we aren't looking for a counter to the complaint. At this moment we aren't trying to justify the price, we are just agreeing, so as to remove a possible conflict. We will deal with how *The Price is a Benefit in* the next lesson.

Here is the second example of how to handle a price objection.

Here again they say something along the lines of

"It's very expensive" or "it's pretty pricey".

Staying calm and without judgement answer with.

"Yes, I agree with you, and I see through the research you have done already that you probably knew that before stopping by today."

Now be careful with this approach. It's effective at getting the client past the complaint, but you must already know their answer. You will know their answer, because you have found it by questioning your client. You should have already learned whether or not they have prior knowledge about your products and services. You should be able to surmise if they already have a good Idea of what they are looking for and know its approximate cost.

Here is some food for thought about complaints. You probably are not the first showroom or website they have visited on this subject. Don't ask them that though. Let them tell you. Never make a liar out of a client. So when they complain, It's just a complaint. They may be fine with the price. They may be fine with the quality. So don't hang on this complaint. First I want you to personally get over it. Then, I want you to get them over it. Just acknowledge the complaint, help them to accept it, and move past it.

Let us finish off this section with a third and final example.

In this scenario we have a client who has come looking for a product. And it's well known that that product they want starts at $1000 and quickly goes up from there. The customer knows this already. They also know that the difference in quality between the $1000 and $10000 version is considerable. They want the higher priced version because of its superior performance. In this scenario we are at a later stage in the conversation. You know the customer wants it, they know they want it. Then this is when they will hit you with a price complaint.

I want you to do this:

Agree with them.

Then encourage them.

Then compliment them.

Then Close them.

So when they say "it's too expensive" or "it's more than i want to spend."

You say this.

"I agree." (Agree)

"Do it anyway." (Encourage)

"You deserve it. You earned it." (Compliment)

"Shall we write it up?" (Close)

See what happened there. You closed down the conflict. You have encouraged them to act. You gave them permission to reward themselves and finally you moved them towards the Close.

So to put this all in perspective. You're selling, and they are buying. Everyone complains about the price. Everyone. But that's why you are here. Whether it's a dollar or a hundred thousand dollars. They are here to buy, and you are here to Close them.

Complaints can be scary. For the unprepared they can bring the sale to a crashing halt, and leave you stammering for a solution to this problem.

However, if you can learn to acknowledge the complaint and then move on from it. You will master your own emotional response, keep control of the sale and keep it moving forward.

# THE PRICE IS A BENEFIT.

In the last section we dealt with the price complaint by acknowledging the client's complaint by agreeing with them and moving on from it. However we were really focusing on you and your own emotional response. Learning to stay cool under pressure.

In this version of dealing with a price objection we will take it up a level. This time we won't try to move on from it, we will confront it head on by acknowledging the price complaint. However this time we will address the complaint by presenting the **Price as the Benefit**.

This time the price is the benefit.

Yes I said that. The price is the benefit. And that is what you are going to present to them, and the fact that **if it was cheaper it wouldn't be as good**.

This is a new take on the old saying "if it was cheap it wouldn't be any good, and good things aren't cheap."

So when they say to you that the price "seems high" or "these sure cost a lot."


You respond like this.

"Yes I agree."

Do not look away when you say this.

"However, the value of it directly reflects the value that they can build into it."

They may not hear you the first time. And they may not understand what you just said. So say it again.

"The value of …. directly reflects the value they can build into it."

Keeping eye contact. Pause and let your words sink in. Now you can explain it to them.

"The high value of …. is how they can build/craft/produce such a high value well designed product"

"The higher value allows for a bigger engineering budget and more choices for the designers to produce a high value, high quality product."

Or another serviced based example would be.

"Yes. The high value of our service is why we can provide the high value services we offer. "

This is a very powerful tool to shut down the complaint. One of my favorite and most successful complaint stoppers.

In the first part you agree with them. Stopping the conflict. ("Yes, I agree")

Then you give them a reason for the price. (The high value of …)

Then finally you justify the high value to them in terms they can understand. ("The higher value allows for a bigger…)

Practice this by repeatedly saying the main part in your head and out loud often, so when you need it, it is right there at the tip of your tongue.

Let's try it one more time together. Shall we.

"The value of …. Is directly reflected in the value of the …."

Remember to use the word "Value". The word **Value** is the key. Emphasize the value.

Never, ever, use "cost" or "price" here. We are providing value to the customer, not a cost.

Be confident in your delivery and you will have success.

# SELL THEM, DON'T LET THEM SELL YOU.

Don't let them sell you.

When I say don't let them sell you. I mean don't let them sell you on their problems. They are not here to sell their problems, they are here to be sold on their wants and desires.

This is an expansion on dealing with complaints.

When you let them sell you their problems. They lose.

When they complain that they don't have enough money, that they don't really need it, they won't be using it that often, or anything else that they say. If you accept what they say as true. Or in other words you buy what they are selling you. They lose getting what they desire, and you lose the sale.

So don't buy it. It's just their rational mind trying to protect their wallet. Help them to move on and towards their desires.

You must continue to treat them as buyers.

Sometimes when a customer tries to sell you on their problems it's a devious way to try to get you to lower the price. Be careful of this type of tactic. Clients use it all the time. They may not even know they are doing it.

It's important for you to control your own emotional response. Don't be afraid of the complaint. Don't you personally buy what they are trying to sell you.

The one you will hear the most often from a customer or a client will involve them starting to downplay their needs.

At this point I want you to remember a very important fact.

They called you. They came to you. They have a desire or need that needs to be filled.

However they will automatically start trying to sell you on the idea that they really don't need the best or that the basic one will do and, why would I need to get the better one when I don't really use it that often.

Ignore these complaints.

It's as if they are trying to downsell themselves, and then trying to downsell you at the same time.

Take note of what they are saying and move forward. Just as with other complaints I will often ignore this tactic or give a minor acknowledgement. Remember if you use your technique properly you will move them up to and or exceed their desired goal. Don't give in. They will thank you.

So remember. Don't let them sell you. If you do, you will fail them.

A final note here. They literally may not have the means to move up a level. But treat them like a buyer with the ability to make a purchase, use proper questioning, and you will find the right answer to their needs. Without giving up profit.

# ALWAYS UPSELL.

Always upsell customers and your clients. I mean this whole heartedly.

Always upsell.

This is a great way to handle a price complaint or a customer's indecision.

I always like to move customers up a level before settling on a product or service. Now you may think that this is risky, considering they may be unsure of the product, or are giving some resistance. It's not a risk, it's an opportunity.

There are many benefits to upselling a client. As it may reveal to you and your client, their true financial ability to pay, both up and down.

The upsell can help a customer to see greater potential, build desire and help them to push themselves to a higher level.

Upselling also strengthens the down sell. As you can use a high priced, higher end product to demonstrate the value of the lower priced product, by connecting the two together through their similar attributes, helping the client feel good about what they are looking at.

Selling up is also good for your ego, it feels good to help a client realize a higher level. They may never have been able to do it without you. Now they have something that they can truly enjoy and benefit from.

And not to mention your career will benefit and your boss or manager will take notice. The rewards can be both financially and spiritually enriching.

So when I have a client and he complains about the price of an Item or is just unsure of the level you are at the moment. I always show them a model up.

When you have the chance to do it, show them more. And to be clear here. They may already like and want the current level of products or service. Then definitely show them what more brings.

Here are some example questions to get the client to take a look.

"Do you want to see what the next level can do?"

"I know it's more than what you came for. However, because you are here, do you want to see it in action?"

"You're here. Before we finish today. For fun. Would you like to see its performance?"

Of course they will say yes.

I never believe that a client can only spend so much. That is them trying to sell you. That is them trying to sell themselves. Sell them. Sell them upward. Bring them upward. And in the end even if they don't buy a bigger package. They will appreciate the value of the one they did go with. There is no down side to upselling.

# DON'T MISS AN OPPORTUNITY.

Remember to keep your eyes and ears open.

Don't miss an opportunity. I can't believe how many times I have witnessed a sales person interacting with a client and they miss an opportunity or miss a chance to expand the opportunity they are in.

When you are presenting to your client, watch for clues. Don't just push through the presentation until you reach the end. You may have a really nice presentation. You may have worked very hard on putting it together. But maybe while presenting it, the client asks you a question that could be the indicator to what they really want. Don't skip over their question. Here is an example of what not to do.

I was sitting in on a presentation. The head designer for the company I was working for at the time was moving through his well put together powerpoint of our company's smart home design capabilities to a group of potential clients. At one point during the presentation, two people in the group asked if our technology could be used in a commercial setting. And just so you know, the answer to their question was Yes.

"Yes it can". That is all he had to say.

But as I stood back watching in horror, the designer, quite frankly, ignored the question and without acknowledgement, moved on with his presentation.

Ignoring the opportunity that had just presented itself, and unable to move away from his notes, a real and clear chance for a much larger job just got up and walked away with the group when he was done.

Had he stopped and addressed their question. Even only to make the point that yes the technology applies and that some of their questions may be answered in the presentation, and that furthermore he would follow up with a deeper look at their question at the end of the presentation. Essentially letting them know he was listening to them. Who knows what kind of work would have come from their inquiry.

A missed opportunity. Keep your ears open.

Another version of not missing the opportunity as it presents itself, comes in the form of you only addressing the clients original question and not seeing the true question.

In this example. The client has come into your establishment looking for X. You have X and know it quite well. But as you are demonstrating X's benefits. Extolling its virtues. You remember your lessons learned so far and ask them a few more questions about what they really want from X.

You may start getting a feeling that they aren't as excited as you think they should be. As they may have been told by friends or the internet that X is what they need. But if you keep trying to sell them X, they will not buy it or they will not be happy with it when they get it home. As it is not what they are really looking for. You could be looking at an unhappy customer and a return.

So while you are engaging with a customer. Keep on the lookout for clues. Often and all of a sudden it may become clear to you.

In this case after some questions, it turns out that Y is what they were looking for all along . Y may be the bigger opportunity, or simply Y is what they really needed, and when they take it home with them, they will keep it.

So remember don't get too focused on the presentation. As they say "Don't miss the forest for the trees."

Remember. Questions are your allies in discovering the client's true wants and desires.

## LET'S TALK TO THE "EXPERT".

Taking your client to talk to an Expert is a very powerful technique to have in your arsenal.

This is one of my favorite ways to deal with a difficult customer who doesn't want to believe you or is resisting your suggestions.

When you are faced with this resistance. Take them to the **Expert**.

The power of the Expert can and will change your customers attitude and the direction your sale is going for the good of you both.

The power of the Expert comes from the introduction.

But let's start at the beginning.

When you meet a customer for the first time, some really negative stereotypes come into play.

Stereotypes, as in, you as a salesperson, are only there to take their money, and you will do anything, including lying to take it from them. This has long been ingrained into the general public psych. Getting over and past it is very difficult.

Don't take it personally. It's just the way it is.

This is where the introduction to the Expert comes in. This is how you defeat this stereotype.

When you meet a customer for the first time and introduce yourself there are perceptions involved and assumptions made. From these perceptions and assumptions, the customer's opinion of you will be made. And that's how they see you.

However if you introduce a person to your customer as an Expert in the subject, that is how the customer will see them.

They won't see them as another salesperson, they will see them as the Expert. Everything the Expert says will be believed as true by the customer, as the Expert is here to inform and his information is free. The Expert is not here to take.

All this power of the Expert coming from a simple introduction.

You will have probably seen this effect before. Think of anytime someone has been introduced to you as a good person, that's probably how you saw them afterwards.

For example.

"Let me introduce you." "Here's Jim, he is a good guy."

Or.

"That there is Jim. He is a good man."

See how it makes you feel. Jim's not even real and you probably feel positive about him.

So let's get back to introducing your customer to the Expert. For best results you should have one or two people you can work with. They could be in sales just like you, they could know exactly what you know on the subject. It helps however if they have a good knowledge on the subject, but what is more important, is that they are new to the customer. When introduced as the Expert, your Expert should know how to act as the Expert. If they know their role they can be prepared mentally.

Let's set up an example here to look at.

So you are in a conversation with a potential client, and you need them to realize that you aren't trying to steal from them, and that you really want them to understand the benefits of a fantastic product.

This is where you bring in the Expert.

Turn to your client and say.

"Lets hold here for a moment." "Would it be ok if I grab Jim?"

Wait just a breath. Then give Jim's credentials.

"Jim is a real expert on this subject. He knows it inside and out. I often turn to him when discussing a client's needs."

Bring Jim into the conversation. Fill him in on what is being discussed, and make the introduction.

"This is Jim. He is an expert. Jim please meet ….."

Now that Jim has been qualified by you as the Expert. They will look at him as an Expert and not a salesman.

This time though, when he ends up basically repeating everything you have discussed already, from him, it will be the truth.

Now that the Expert has confirmed everything. Your previous words will have become true.

Your customer will see you differently and be more open to you.

Learn to use the Expert. Practice it. Be prepared to use it. You will come to rely on it.

# BECAUSE.

BECAUSE. Now this is a terribly powerful word. I say terrible because it can be used for good or for evil. It can be used to manipulate or to give a push in the right direction. If used correctly with good morals and empathy it can have a dramatic effect on your client and whether or not they Close on a sale.

This word, if used correctly can have a big effect on your career.

I learned to use the word **Because** as a sales technique later in my sales career. After all, I had learned over the years about customer interaction, and the practice of good customer service. Learning to use "BECAUSE" was a real eye opener into the effects that words can have on a person.

Because.

Where it began for me. While reading a book on psychology I came across research on the word. There was a very interesting experiment that used the word Because to affect the outcome of a situation. Here are the basics of that experiment.

As it goes the experiment was set up to see the effect of words used to get a certain result.

In the experiment a person would wait in line for a photocopier. They would ask those in front of them if they could go to the front of the line. And generally no matter how nicely or forcefully they asked they were turned down. When the question to move to the front of the line was started with "**Because**". They were often allowed without resistance to move to the front.

Where before the experimenter would ask.

"I am late, may I skip ahead to make some copies."

They would stand about a 50/50 chance on whether or not they encountered pushback for their request. But when they changed the question to.

"Because I am late, may I make my copies now."

They would have a much much higher chance of being allowed to make their copies without any push back.

Furthermore, in the experiment. And this was the part that really made the power of the word **Because** apparent. They would ask the question but with no excuse or request for sympathy. The experimenter would just simply ask.

"Because I have to make copies, can I go now?"

And the effect it had on those waiting ahead would be the same. They would allow the researcher to move forward to make their copies.

So after reading this I started to try **BECAUSE** as a Closing statement.

"Because it's time, shall we write this up?"

It had an immediate effect on the conversation. Where before, sometimes I would try two or three official Closes to conclude the transaction. Now we would move directly to settling up. The word has power.

From that point forward, after what I thought was the end of the questions, and I thought the customer was educated enough. I would Close with a **Because** statement such as.

"Because you are here, shall we do this?"

Or

"Because it's time to move forward with your project whose name shall I put on the bill."

Using Because would have a great effect on moving the customer to action.

So, use Because regularly to move a customer towards taking home their wants and desires. You will be rewarded.

## TRY ONE MORE TIME.

To finish off the Advanced Techniques section, I want you to do something for yourself.

I want you to try one more time.

If they haven't Closed on their desire.
If they are walking away.
If they just won't commit.

Try one more time!

I find that sales people will not try one more time to make the sale. They let the sale walk.

How many times should you try one more time?
As many tries as it takes.
Try again. Ask again.
Be brave.

Read this lesson again.
Ok. Let's move on.

# SECTION 6: PRICE NEGOTIATIONS

In this next section we will look at dealing with price negotiation. Our focus though won't be the haggling over price.

Our focus here will be to help the client with their struggle to accept the price.

We will help them to accept it. We will help their logical side, the side of their mind that is protecting the wallet. We help them to give into their desire, open the wallet and make the investment.

I want to say to you here. At this point if you have done your work. Asked the questions. Built the desire. Forged the trust with your customer. The push to get them to Close should be met with little resistance.

Remember. They have come to you, because they have a want, a desire to be filled.

So let's take a look at some techniques.

# WHEN POSSIBLE, NEGOTIATE BY MOVING DOWN A PRODUCT LINE.

Sometimes a client is asking for too much discount or just simply complaining too much about the price.

Don't just give in to make a sale.

Don't give away your profit.

Don't give up on price.

It's time to move them down a level.

But first, as we have already learned. Move them up a level. Show them what is possible. Then show them what they lose, and what they keep by going to the bottom level. It will help them to stay with the current model.

Their mind will come to grips with the choice. And ease them into making the investment.

This works on the good, better, best principle. People will usually go for the middle. Their mind will settle on it as the best solution.

So again. Don't be afraid to move down a level before giving up on price and profit.

Negotiate with product not money.

## REDUCE A CLIENT'S FEAR OF MONEY. MAKE IT EASY FOR THE CLIENT TO BUY.

Often referred to as Reduce to the Ridiculous or Reduce to the Penny. This approach is a great way to help remove the customer's fear of taking money out of their wallet. Reducing their fear of the financial commitment.

The idea here is to reduce the cost of the purchase to zero over time.

If a customer has a complaint. A fear. Attack their fear by breaking down the cost over time.

First by the year, then by the month, then by the week, then by the day.

Let's take an item that has a price of $5000 for example. And we will use 5 years as the length of time.

The customer says to you something like "Five thousand seems like a lot."

Respond with "Yes, however let's look at it over five years and see what it really means."

First reduce by year.

"Over five years it's only a thousand a year."

Then by month.

"And by the month it's eighty three dollars and thirty three cents."

Then by the week.

"By the week it would only be twenty dollars and eighty three cents."

Then by the day

"So what I am saying is, it is two dollars and ninety seven cents a day."

"Are you really concerned about two dollars and ninety seven cents a day? You will spend more than that on your coffee."

See what's happening here. We are taking it down to a ridiculous level. Reducing the fear to nothing. Sure, $5000 could feel like a big cost, but $2.97. That's nothing. What's to fear about $2.97?

I have even heard it said that you can break it down even further by the hour or minute. Do whatever it takes. You can even add family members to the equation by dividing the time by their use also. Take that $2.97 down to pennies if you have to.

It works. This should be high in your repertoire.

Set a reasonable amount of time with your client or customer. Remember to ask them questions about their use and get to work reducing the fear. The more their rational side can reconcile the expense, the easier it becomes for them to invest.

Over the years I have developed a version of this I like to use.

In this version of reducing the cost to the ridiculous, I will ask them leading questions to establish a time. Questions like.

"How long did you own the last one for?"

Or

"How long did you own your last car(replace with something appropriate) for?"

When they answer, I use the time they have provided to quickly reduce their fear of the cost. Here are some examples that work well.

"It's been ten years?" "Do you even remember what you paid for it back then?"

Or

"Ten years. It's given you ten years of enjoyment?" I will let them answer and or just let it sink in. Then follow up with. "When you have this one for another ten years will you even care what you invested for ten years worth of enjoyment today?"

Or

"In ten years Will you even remember what you spent?"

Or

"You will have owned two cars by the time you have owned this for 10 years.". My favorite response from the customer here is when they say it may be more than two.

Use these. Mix them up as you need. Get the customer past the price. Reduce the fear. Help them to acquire their desire.

# CREATE VALUE. JUSTIFY WITH A FINANCIAL VALUE MULTIPLIER.

Increase the value of the customer's wants by adding another piece that will multiply its value and performance.

Creating value with a financial value multiplier is a great way to help a customer see a product or service in a new positive and more attractive way. And not just as an extra expense. Especially if you are trying to add the benefit of one product to another product. Here is the basic idea.

The client is here for X. X is worth $1000. You are also trying to sell the client B. B is worth $100. B will vastly improve the performance of X. The issue stopping the client from Closing on B is that X will operate without it. Even if at this moment the client believes that B could be a benefit. The client is having a hard time justifying the extra cost of B. Their wallet is closing up.

At the moment, all they see is a bigger bill. $1000 + $100. Since you are adding B and X does not need B to function. B is just an option.

Let's help them justify the extra expense. And get that performance they deserve.

What you want to help them to understand is that B is not an extra expense. B is a Multiplier of performance. And the true value of B plus X is not $1100. The true value of the extra expense is X multiplied by B.

Please note that you will have to give B a multiplier value that makes sense in your particular situation. Don't get to carried away. Or you risk losing the clients trust.

Here is an example of how to sell the client on the benefits of adding B.

The customer is resisting. Say this.

"It's a multiplier of performance."

They may ask you to explain yourself. Follow up with this explanation.

"Think of it like this."

"Let's use a dollar value to represent performance."

"When you add B to X. You are not increasing the value of X by $100."

"The effect that B will have on X, is a multiplier of performance. So instead of X providing a thousand dollars of performance. It will perform like it's worth five thousand dollars. Well beyond its base level."

"Now imagine having that at home."

What you now have done is justified the extra expense. They don't have to purchase a $5000 product to get that level of performance. By spending a little extra they save $3900 and receive all of the performance.

You have justified for them, the investment in themselves.

Learn this one. It works. Practice your delivery so that it is smooth and without hesitation.

# I HAVE NO MORE MONEY TO GIVE YOU.

Ok, this one is a little aggressive. It's a hardline technique for dealing with clients that keep asking for more and more discount, and you need them to move on to making a final decision.

You say it just like this.

"I have no more money to give you."

Don't explain yourself. It will just weaken your position. What you just said is the explanation.

You gave them all the money you could. And who doesn't like being given money.

Now they know they are not over paying and getting your best price. It should snap them back on track.

It's here that you may find that it's out of their range, or better yet, they are ready to move forward.

Go for the Close or move to a different offering they have the means to acquire.

This one takes some guts. So be bold.

# SECTION 7: CLOSES

## Intensify Buying Desire With Great Closes.

This is a fun section. I have always enjoyed using great **Closes** while working with a customer.

It has always amazed me how you can see the effect of a well worded Closing statement on a customer. Watching the desire in them build or moving them right to the final acquisition.

Below are some fantastic **Closing** phrases for you to use when helping your customer or client acquire their wants and desires.

Use these all through your time with the client. Use them individually or weave them together. Have fun with them. Here we go.

# SHALL WE?

**"Shall we write it up?"**

**"Shall we fill out the paperwork?"**

**"Shall we write this up?"**

These are fantastic. They help to Close by moving the client in a positive way towards the Close without mentioning money. Remember the money is still in the wallet safe. There is no mention of purchasing. There is no asking if they would like to buy it. What is so good about "Shall we write this up" is the absence of money in that phrase. When you are writing something up. You aren't asking them to pay for anything. You are not asking for them to pay a price. You are simply writing it up.

# WHO'S NAME?

**"Who's name is going on the paperwork?"**

**"Who's name shall we put on it?"**

**"Who's name are we writing this up with?"**

As with the previous "Shall we write it up" Closes, these again move the client towards the Close by helping them to take ownership without the mentioning of money.

Try combining "Who's name" and "Shall we write it up" for a terrific merging of the two expressions.

Ask them.

**"Who's name are we putting on this?"**

When they answer with a name follow up with.

**"Shall we write it up?"**

The combo works well to help them establish ownership, and it moves them to the Close, all without money being mentioned.

# GO FOR IT!

**"Go for it! What do you have to lose?"**

This time we are telling the client to take action to get what they want, like it says, let them know to Go For it. This should be used later in the conversation at a point when you have learned more about your client. You should know the answer to this before you ask it. But when used at the right moment it will Close a client.

# TREAT YOURSELF.

**"Treat yourself. You deserve it"**

**"Treat yourself. You've earned it"**

**"You deserve it."**

Another good Close. It deals with a couple of situations. One when running into the price complaint or two when dealing with a hesitating customer. "Treat yourself, you deserve it" directly attacks the clients desires. Helping the side of their brain that feels the desire, to override the side that is protecting the wallet. They might just realize they do deserve it.

# DO IT ANYWAY.

**"Do it anyway."**

Again you are just helping them over the hump of hesitation that everyone feels when making a decision. Be encouraging.

# YOU CANT TAKE IT WITH YOU.

**"You can't take it with you."**

This one works. Have courage. This goes right to the point. When you are gone you're gone, so enjoy it now while you can.

# HAVEN'T YOU ALREADY THOUGHT ABOUT IT?

**"Haven't you already thought about it? And that's why you are here. It's time to stop shopping and start enjoying."**

This is a response for when the customer says they have to think about it. Look right at them when you say it and wait for their response. Say it again if you have to.

# BECAUSE.

"Because you are here. Shall we write this up?"

"Because it's time, shall we write this up?"

"Because it's time to move forward with your project whose name shall I put on the bill!"

Review the section on the word **Because** to understand the psychology behind its power.

Close with a **"Because"** to move the client to act on acquiring their wants and needs. You will also find that **Because** can be mixed with many of the other Closes presented here. For example.

"Because you deserve it."

"Because you can't take it with you. Do it anyway."

"Because you've earned it."

# I UNDERSTAND.

**"I understand. Can you share with me your concern?"**

A good question to uncover the root of their hesitation. If it's a small concern that can be handled easily. Address the concern. Ask for the Close.

# ASK FOR FORGIVENESS.

**"It's better to ask for forgiveness than ask for permission."**

An oldie but a goodie. Use it. It works. Plus it is fun to see their reactions.

# WHY?

**"Why would you buy that?"**

**"Why are you looking at that?"**

**"Why is this one the right choice?"**

These Closes do the work for you. Getting the client to tell you about their reasons for wanting your product or service strengthens their desire. After they move through their reasons. Ask for the Close.

# YOUR MONEY IS SAFE IN YOUR WALLET.

**"Your money is safe in your wallet. It's my job to help you use it."**

This is a powerful Closing statement to help break down a client's resistance to pulling the trigger on a sale and opens them up to the realization that you are here to help them and not to just take from them. It works by making an outlandish statement, usually followed by a look of shock from the customer, and an explanation from you that sets them free.

First let's look at what this statement implies and what is really being said.

I am doing my job.

I am here to help you.

Your money is safest in your wallet.

But you want something.

It is my job to help you spend your money.

It's my responsibility to help you get your needs and desires.

Let's get this done.

As you can see there is a lot packed into a simple statement. I call it the **Your money is safest in your wallet Close**. This one has been a favorite of mine for sometime now.

First a little backstory about this one. I am not sure what got me to try it the first time. I mean it's a crazy thing for a salesperson to say to a customer. But I do remember the dramatic effect it had on my client. At that time they were looking at a really expensive pair of stereo speakers. I mean really expensive. But the sale was starting to stall. We were deep into our time together, and I had done what I was supposed to do up to this point. Questioning him, building rapport, finding his true desire and strengthening it, but there we were. He was stalling out and backing away from the sale. Admittedly I was a little desperate, as I did not want to lose this one. That's when it came out of me. I looked at him and explained my duty to him. It went something like this.

"Look, I am just doing my job here. I am trying to help you."

"See. Your money is safe right now. And will be safe as long as you don't do anything. But that's not why you are here."

"So my job is to help you use your money to get what you want."

"If I don't do that I will fail you in this."

And that did it. It was really satisfying to have him say.

"Let's write it up."

What a moment that was.

It was fairly long winded the first time. Later I shortened the delivery to just.

"Your money is safe in your wallet. It's my job to help you spend it."

The customer. Shocked. May ask.

**"What do you mean?"**

Say it again and let it sink in.

**"Your money is safe in your wallet. It's my job to help you spend it and get things you want."**

Be confident when you use this one and it will deliver for you. The customer has to believe that you are acting as their fiduciary, working in their best interest. When I use it, it is often near the end of our time together. However as I have become more confident in its use, I have moved it closer and closer to the beginning of an interaction with a customer. When I use it though. It's because I know it will kick a customer out of park and into gear. By saying it, it helps them to shed their fear of spending the money and to make an exchange.

## SUMMARY

Now at the end of all of this. It's time for you to become a master of your craft. I encourage you to read and read the different lessons. Ideally I would love for you to be able to completely internalize the theories and techniques presented in this manual by simply reading them. But in reality you have to go out into the field to sharpen your skills. With practice you can and will calibrate the techniques to your own personal style. You will learn to master yourself and become a master at motivating your customers to Close on their desires.

So don't wait. Start today. Do not delay.

If I come to you for a watch or a new suit. I want to leave with a better watch than I told myself I was going to buy. I want my new suit to be finer and more luxurious than I told myself I deserve.

I hate poorly delivered sales pitches. Practice. It's your job to help me get my true desire. Do not let me down.

Believe in your own greatness. As I believe in you.

# AFTERWORD

Thank you for taking your personal time to read Stop Selling and Start Closing. If you have questions or need clarification in any of the lessons please reach out to me at michaelwsteiger@gmail.com.

Michael W Steiger

www.ingramcontent.com/pod-product-compliance
Lightning Source LLC
Chambersburg PA
CBHW062224080426
42734CB00010B/2014